BEETHOVEN'S SKETCHES

BEETHOVEN'S SKETCHES

AN ANALYSIS OF HIS STYLE BASED ON A STUDY OF HIS SKETCH-BOOKS

By PAUL MIES

Translated by
DORIS L. MACKINNON

DOVER PUBLICATIONS, INC.
NEW YORK

Published in Canada by General Publishing Company, Ltd., 30 Lesmill Road, Don Mills, Toronto, Ontario.

Published in the United Kingdom by Constable and Company, Ltd., 10 Orange Street, London WC 2.

International Standard Book Number: 0-486-23042-2
Library of Congress Catalog Card Number: 73-88334

Manufactured in the United States of America
Dover Publications, Inc.
180 Varick Street
New York, N.Y. 10014

TO MY WIFE
LOUISE

CONTENTS

Introduction 1

PART I. STYLE DETERMINANTS

I. The melodic line:

   (a) Up-beat and 'curtain' . . . 5
   (b) The melodic apex and its treatment . 16
   (c) Repetition of notes 35
   (d) Suspension: absolute melodic structure . 39

II. The melodic form:

   (a) The types of melody . . . 44
   (b) Threefold repetition . . . 46
   (c) Avoidance of sequences and uniform rhythms; characteristic relations between the melodic types, and their changes . 56
   (d) Sequence-contractions . . . 76
   (e) Transformation of the types . . 85
   (f) Themes with irregular number of bars . 101
   (g) Melodic breadth and elimination of caesurae 102
   (h) The fugue theme 110

III. Unity within the movement and in the complete works, whether considered singly or in groups:

   (a) Relations within the movement and within the work 114
   (b) Relations within a group of works . . 123

IV. Constant features in the development:

   (a) Constancy in the treatment of motive and rhythm 131
   (b) Modulation 137
   (c) Instrumentation 141
   (d) General plans 141

PART II

V. Beethoven as creative artist:
    (a) Writing the sketches . . . 147
    (b) Artistic creation 149
    (c) Aesthetic judgement . . . 154
    (d) The importance of the sketches to Beethoven 157

PART III. THE MUSICAL EXPRESSION

VI. Beethoven as composer of instrumental music and as writer of songs. . . . 162

VII. Style features adopted for their expressive value:
    (a) The common chord and other structures in the melody 165
    (b) Suspension and descending seconds . . 167
    (c) 'Ornament' 170
    (d) 'Character' of the keys . . . 174
    (e) Notation and musical expression . . 182

Conclusion 187
List of Abbreviations 189
Bibliography 189
List of Works cited 191
Index of Names 195

INTRODUCTION

' . . . To write the history of Beethoven's inner and outer life would be a wonderful undertaking.' [1] Thus Schumann wrote in the year 1838. And perhaps no other musician offers conditions so favourable for the study of his inner history (i.e. the growth of the musical ideas, motives, themes and completed works). Writers have been quick to see this. Special mention must be made of G. Nottebohm, who, in a large number of works, opened Beethoven's sketch-books to us and therewith the composer's inner history—a most laborious task, in view of the almost illegible nature of much of the manuscript. Schumann's idea,[2] that genius must be aided by a will of iron, might have been expressed with special reference to these sketch-books. For, through them, it is often possible to trace, step by step, how the most sublime melodies take origin in something very simple. It is often said that Beethoven's 'daemoniacal constructive power'[3] always succeeded in getting the best end-result from what he had sketched. 'And though these sketches not infrequently give an impression of hesitation and groping, our admiration revives at sight of this power of self-criticism, brought to the pitch of genius; and we marvel at the way in which, after everything has been tested, it confidently retains that which is best. I have had the opportunity of examining not a few of Beethoven's sketch-books; but I have never come across an instance where I was not bound to admit that what he selected was really the most beautiful.'[4] 'One cannot but be struck by the

[1] *Briefe*, Neue Folge, II. Aufl., p. 122.
[2] *Gesammelte Schriften* (P. Reclam, vol. iii, p. 126).
[3] H. Schenker, *Erläuterungsausgabe zur Sonate Op.* 111, p. 64.
[4] O. Jahn, *Gesammelte Aufsätze über Musik*, p. 244.

way in which Beethoven's admirable artistic instinct infallibly selects from out a mass of sketches the best reading.'[1]

And Nottebohm (N. ii, p. ix)[2] lays stress on the importance of these sketches for 'the history of his evolution as an artist'. In his first publication (N. 65, p. 7) he says: 'Once it is shown that Beethoven never moved in a rut (and how else would one describe his independence of any conventional method of procedure?) it is obvious that we shall not discover from the sketch-books what was the inner law that guided him in his creative work.' By this Nottebohm meant that Beethoven sometimes sketched out a large plan as the commencement, and sometimes began with the detail. And clearly he was thinking of the same thing when later (N. ii, p. lx) he wrote: 'What one sees in Beethoven's sketch-books occurs over and over again: and it would be so much waste effort to repeat the same remark or explanation with regard to each of the sketches, thrown out, as they are, now in one direction and now in another.' More recent investigators, whose endeavour has been to penetrate so far as possible the idiosyncrasies of Beethoven's musical style, have taken up one instance or another from the sketch-books, and from these have drawn important conclusions as regards the final form and the other works. Gal[2] (pp. 60, 72), for instance, through a comparison of this kind, has revealed the infrequency of suspensions and of chromaticism in Beethoven's music, the result of which is an idiosyncrasy of the melody to which he gives the name 'absolute'. Becking[2] (pp. 128, 137, 140) has shown what the special features of Beethoven's scherzo theme are, and with what sureness these were developed from sketches that at first were framed quite differently.

[1] M. Friedländer, *Jahrbuch der Musikbibliothek Peters*, 14. Jahrg. p. 19.
[2] See list of abbreviations.

Such examples, however, deal with isolated instances from the sketch-books, and not with a comparison drawn from the wealth of material which these contain. Again and again [1] I have insisted that, while a single instance may be of great interest, yet, for determining points of style, it is of immense value to collect together a number of such instances and make a comparison between them. If one carefully goes through the sketch-books published by Nottebohm, one sees that actually a number of groups can be formed, in which similar alterations were made on the original drafts: as, for instance, where melodies lacking an up-beat were given one, or where melodies of a certain form were re-shaped although the main motive was retained; and so forth. We are justified in concluding that to Beethoven the final reading represented an advance on the sketches, and that it is in the final selection that the individual features of his style will therefore be most fully expressed. The direction of the alteration draws our attention to the points that Beethoven's musical sense selected as the best. The laws governing his art are thus revealed; these are the style determinants that must be grasped. In a special section (II) we shall consider to what extent the alterations were made with deliberate intent, and to what extent they were unconscious. In addition to noting the similarity of the changes that he made, it is well worth while to observe what Beethoven chose to retain. For these must also be things that he thought good and valuable and in correspondence with his ideas as an artist: by studying them we may get a further clue to his musical idiosyncrasy.

The following study is based on this line of argument. The main material is taken from the four works [2] published by Nottebohm. I have also, of course, drawn on other sources, such as Schenker's editions, Thayer's

[1] P. Mies, *Stilmomente und Ausdrucksstilformen im Brahmsschen Lied*, p. 3.
[2] See list of abbreviations.

biography,[1] &c. It is obvious, and indeed inevitable, that a number of the conclusions I submit here must coincide with those of other investigators who have interested themselves in Beethoven's style (Gal, Fischer,[1] Jalowetz,[1] Becking [1]): the researches of these authors, since they are based on the completed work, must necessarily include these points of style, which, in the present work, are indicated by the alterations and retentions. The use of Nottebohm's works instead of the original sketch-books imposes a certain restriction; for while Nottebohm noted the essential points concerning the themes and the alterations made in these, it was only in the sketch-book devoted to the Eroica (N. 80) that he enlarged on the changes in the working-out, etc. In this essay, style idiosyncrasies are determined according as Beethoven altered or retained his initial idea. This limitation is necessary: there is the difficulty in interpreting the sketch-books; and, still more important, the fact that, even where one can do so, a general view of the manifold phenomena they reveal is not easy. Now, for such a study as I propose, this wide and continuous survey is just what is necessary. I believe, however, that, by the method I have adopted, I have succeeded in tracing to their objective foundations the essential peculiarities of Beethoven's melodic structure.

[1] See list of abbreviations.

I

THE MELODIC LINE

(a) Up-beat and 'curtain'.

FISCHER (p. 50) has emphasized the importance in the Viennese classical style of the lively up-beat, combined with sustained endings to the motives. As a matter of fact, in the sketch-books there are a large number of instances in which melodies, originally without up-beat, are given one later on. It is at once obvious that Beethoven attached importance to up-beats of this kind; otherwise he would not have changed the original ideas. The reasons for inserting an up-beat are several. Frequently all that had to be done was to impart greater movement and tension to an existing up-beat. There is an example of this in the piano sonata Op. 90:

It is also to be noted here that at first the melodic line began with the repetition of a note. Later on I shall show in more detail that Beethoven preferred to avoid such repetitions. So the up-beat G sharp was changed to E, F sharp. The same thing is shown by the change in the up-beat in No. 2 of the song-cycle Op. 98:

Wo die Ber - ge so blau

Op. 98.

Wo die Ber - ge so blau aus dem ne - bli - gen Grau

Here the harmonisation shows something further: to the key of G its dominant D has been prefixed. This makes the up-beat more tense, and forces it towards the principal key. Sonata Op. 22 also shows a deliberate emphasizing of the dominant in the up-beat. Moreover, by this device Beethoven avoids having the first note of the melody as apex: I shall return to this point later.

3. N. II. p. 379.

Sonata Op. 22.

Allegretto.

Often this tension in the dominant is evidently Beethoven's reason for introducing an up-beat in a tune that previously lacked it.[1] One of the most striking examples is the trio in the minuet of the eighth symphony. Ex. 4 gives the process of evolution; only in the final form does the up-beat C, D, E occur, whereby the dominant C major obviously imparts tension to the beginning.

4. N. II. p. 115.
Trio.

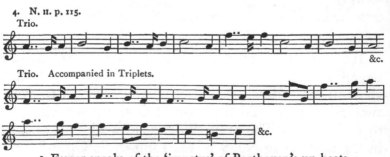

&c.

Trio. Accompanied in Triplets.

&c.

[1] Essner speaks of the 'impetus' of Beethoven's up-beats.

Trio.

Eighth Symphony.[1]

Much the same requirement has produced the up-beat in the theme of the cello sonata Op. 102. 1.

5. N. II. p. 316.
Fugue.

Sonata Op. 102. 1.

The adagio in the quartet in E flat major, Op. 127, shows the same sort of thing. The theme in A flat major, originally without up-beat, is given one by the

notes , in which again the dominant prevails. At the same time, the melody receives two introductory bars on the dominant seventh—a 'curtain', to use Riemann's [2] terminology.

And these brief 'curtains' which appear, especially in the later works, in melodies originally without up-beat, must have seemed to Beethoven of great importance: in the sketches they often do not occur at all. I would instance the theme of the allegro appassionato in the A minor quartet, Op. 132. Beethoven often began thus: he even thought of using it for the finale of the ninth symphony. Ex. 6 brings together some sketches, the second of which has an up-beat, and the final version a two-bar curtain over tonic and dominant. The eight-

[1] Concerning the reading of this bar see Müller-Reuter, *Lexikon der deutschen Konzertliteratur*, Nachtrag zu Bd. I, p. 31.

[2] H. Riemann, *System der musikalischen Rhythmik und Metrik*, p. 230.

7

bar introduction to the scherzo of the ninth symphony
was later added to it as well.

6a. N. II. p. 180. July (?) 1823.
Finale instrumentale.

6b. N. II. p. 180.

6c. N. II. p. 181. Autumn 1823.

Op. 132, 1824/25.

In both cases the actual melody is without up-beat.
And a well-known instance is that of the interpolation
of the initial bar in the slow movement of Op. 106,
where the dominant is indicated by the note C sharp.
Of the effect of this one bar, F. Ries (Leitzmann,[1]
I, p. 76) tells us: 'A very striking thing, from the artistic
standpoint, happened in the case of ... Op. 106, which,
when engraved, is 41 pages in length.... When the en-
graving was finished, and I was daily expecting a letter
fixing the date of publication, I got one with nothing

---

[1] See list of abbreviations.

in it but the following remarkable instruction, "at the beginning of the Adagio" (which, when engraved, occupies

9–10 pages) "insert these two notes— ".

I was to add two notes to a work that had been elaborated in every detail and finished six months before. But I was equally astonished at the effect these two notes produced.' It is not mere chance that, among the examples Riemann gives in the chapter on 'curtains', Beethoven's later works are especially numerous: it was only in his more mature years that he became such a master in the art of creating the right atmosphere by the simple device of using an up-beat containing the dominant chord.

The re-shaping of the up-beat in Op. 22 (Ex. 3) shows that Beethoven tried to avoid having an apex at the beginning of the melody. We should not be justified in drawing this conclusion from a single instance, but there are other indications of the same kind. We frequently find that melodies originally written without up-beat, and having their highest note at the beginning, were later modified by the introduction of an up-beat in a lower register. The opening bars of the last movement of the piano sonata Op. 27. 1 will illustrate this:

7. N. II. p. 250.

Op. 27. 1.

&c.

The dominant up-beat B flat is added to the original draft seemingly quite arbitrarily. It is interesting to notice also that in none of the concluding sections of this movement is the up-beat quaver treated in an unusual way—a clear sign that it was inserted afterwards; and often in the course of the movement the theme comes in without it. The alteration in the melody of the variations in Op. 18. v belongs to the same category:

8. N. ii. p. 490.

Op. 18. v.

By avoiding the first, schematic form of the melody, the highest note came near the beginning; in the later working-out, where the thematic material is otherwise very similar, an up-beat was inserted first. The alterations in the opening themes of the sonata Op. 106 and of the quartet Op. 131 show the same thing.

9. N. ii. p. 123.
Allegro molto.

Op. 106.

10. N. ii. p. 7.

Op. 131.

In the last example, probably on account of the chromaticism, it was important to prepare the way for the apex even more effectively than was done in the sketch. And the addition of the 'curtain' to the slow movement of Op. 106, mentioned on p. 10, may have the same object. In all these examples, the intention is to avoid beginning with the highest note of the melody, which might too easily be felt as the climax. The beginning of Op. 106 (Ex. 9) shows this clearly. Nottebohm also was struck by the change in the second theme in the last movement of Op. 53. The crotchet C became a repeated quaver, and from that the actual up-beat was derived.

11.   N. 80. p. 65.

Op. 53.

The change in the mood is especially clear in this example.

At the same time, in this theme he avoids a halt in the melody and the obvious effect of the repeated note by breaking up the first crotchet into two quavers, and by the caesura after the first quaver, as the result of the up-beat. A halt in the melody may be produced by a rest, and Beethoven prefers to change such pauses into up-beats. The second theme in Sonata Op. 10. III illustrates a case of the kind:

12.   N. II. p. 37.

Op. 10. III.

In this example also the apex of the melody comes

early. In other places Beethoven merely fills in the rests and does not add the up-beat at the beginning. Thus, in the violin sonata Op. 30. III:

13. N. 65. p. 29.

Op. 30. III.

The same thing is beautifully illustrated in the three-fold recurrence of the adagio melody in the serenade Op. 8, and in the first theme of the rondo of the string trio Op. 9. II. But it should be noticed that, in the last example from Op. 30. III, 8, 9. II, the apex of the melody is placed further from the beginning than in the previous ones. The three repetitions from Op. 8:

14. Serenade Op. 8.

Adagio. &c.   Tempo I. &c.

Adagio. &c.

show admirably the development towards an increasing dominant-tendency in the up-beat. To the same category belongs the up-beat to the second part of 'Adelaide', the late addition of which surely no one would have suspected.

15. N. II. p. 536.

&c.

Adelaide.

Einst, o Wun-der! o Wun-der! ent-blüht auf mei-nem Gra-be &c.

Here also it is obvious that Beethoven intended to fill in the second rest, and so was led to the up-beat. The up-beat does not correspond to the rhythm of the verse: further on, I shall frequently have occasion to point out such 'instrumental' influences in the vocal music. A phrase from the theme of the funeral march of the Eroica shows the same thing, and something additional. Originally the phrase ran as in Ex. 16 a. In a later sketch *one* up-beat was introduced (Ex. 16 b), no doubt merely to fill in the rest. But this meant that the two sequences were now different; in the final version an up-beat is inserted in the middle, and, in a higher register, repeats the first up-beat in intensified form.

16 a. N. 80. p. 38.

16 b. N. 80. p. 39.

16 c. Third Symphony.

Among the reasons for introducing the up-beat here is the intention of getting greater roundness and symmetry into the form. Many further examples can be brought to illustrate this point. The second theme of the first movement of the violin sonata

13

Op. 30. II originally had the form Ex. 17 a; the next form (Ex. 17 b) introduces the up-beat when the theme (expanded now from four bars to eight) is repeated; and thence the final reading sets it directly at the beginning.

We must interpret the elongation by syncopation of the initial quaver in the beautiful andante melody of the slow movement of the ninth symphony as having, formally, a similar significance; for each bar overlaps the next with an up-beat (semiquaver or quaver). This syncopated up-beat results in the syncopated binding of the bars that follow, and repeated notes are thereby avoided. An experiment following the above in the sketch-book shows that Beethoven actually had this avoidance in mind (Ex. 18 c). But it destroyed the peaceful beauty of the passage: the solution finally selected is undoubtedly both the simplest and the richest in feeling.

18 c. N. II. p. 176.

18 d. Ninth Symphony.

The theme of the A minor quartet, Op. 132, is an instructive example of how the up-beat character of the later segments has an effect in a backward direction. At first the sketches (Ex. 19 a) show it without initial up-beat; it is obvious that the later bars have an up-beat. Then at the beginning it acquires an up-beat (Ex. 19 b); in the next sketch this up-beat is cut out, with a sequential continuation (Ex. 19 c); in a later experiment (Ex. 19 d), the second part of the sequence again has an up-beat—the pause on G sharp was obviously too long. Finally, the last reading (Ex. 19 e) reverts to the first plan, but the beginning is given the force of an up-beat.

19 a. N. II. p. 547.

19 b.

19 c.

19 d.

19 e. Op. 132.

15

I consider that the instances cited (and I might give many more of the kind) show that Beethoven added up-beats to the original ideas for the following reasons: to avoid repetition of notes, to prepare the apex of the melody, and to clarify and round off the form. To what degree this was conscious or unconscious does not concern us here: all we have to do is to demonstrate the fact. These phenomena fall into two classes; in the one, the principle and object is the alteration of the melodic line; in the other, it is the shaping of the form. The distribution of the up-beats contributes to the establishment of the form, and their dominant character brings out the tonality more clearly. The beginning of the trio in the eighth symphony (Ex. 4) constitutes thus a much better cut between the main movement and the trio than it would without an up-beat: the form is made much clearer. These two aims appear again and again in a number of alteration groups. As the next peculiarity, let us deal with the position of the melodic apex.

(b) *The melodic apex and its treatment.*

The position of the melodic apex is of great importance for the effect of the melody. Naumann[1] has demonstrated certain laws bearing on this point—for instance, as regards the ancient classical fugue theme; and I have been able to confirm and apply these rules to a particular instance (the fugue based on the name of Bach).[2] In the present connexion I take the apex to be, not the highest note of the whole melody, but merely the highest note of a large portion, clearly delimited by sequence or cadence; unimportant auxiliary notes, grace-notes, etc. may be higher still, though for the most part these are only seconds.

[1] E. Naumann, *Darstellung eines bisher unbekannt gebliebenen Stilgesetzes im Aufbau des klassischen Fugenthemas*, 1878.
[2] *Die Kraft des Themas, dargestellt an B-A-C-H*, Bach-Jahrbuch, 1922, p. 14.

In comparing the sketches, several types of treatment can be demonstrated, by the aid of which Beethoven devised an effective position for the melodic apex. In Part I we have seen examples showing how, by its tension, a lower up-beat, usually in the dominant, prepares the way for the apex (Exs. 3, 7, 8, 9, 10, 11). It was Beethoven's custom to strengthen the thematic material and effect of early apices by immediate repetition of the first motive, often in a higher register. The technique of the sequences in Beethoven's melody is one of the points already most often noted, and we shall go into it in detail later on. The sequences under notice are remarkable for their brevity, and consist almost exclusively of two segments. A characteristic example is the beginning of the violin sonata Op. 24, which has the highest note coming first with a one-bar sequence.

20. Op. 24.

The rondo melody of Op. 22 (Ex. 3) also belongs here: with the change in the up-beat the apex was removed from the beginning; there is a two-bar sequence. Ex. 21a gives the minuet melody of the eighth symphony as first sketched. Two things were altered, which have relation to the high note's position so near the beginning. Here, where we have to do with the eight-bar song type, we can scarcely speak of a repetition of sequences; nevertheless, a strengthening is constantly effected in this way. At first the apex lay in the up-beat: that was changed. And finally an ascending two-bar 'curtain' was also inserted.

21a. N. II. p. 114.

Ex. 21 b gives the final version. It is easy to find numerous instances of the kind in the completed works. Of greater importance to us here are those places in the sketches where the actual steps towards such repetitions are elucidated. In the first draft for the presto melody of Op. 18. III (Ex. 22 a) the theme opens with the high note on the unaccented part of the bar; the movement is so quick that the effect of the sequence of the first four half-bars is not great.

22 a. N. II. p. 477.

The final reading (Ex. 22 b) shows the progress to the short sequence of two segments of four bars, as a result of the tempo. In addition, the high note is repeated in the accented part of the bar.

22 b. Op. 18. III.

The alterations in the finale of Op. 59. II follow the same tendency. The two first drafts (Exs. 23 a and b)

18

have the high note at the beginning, and no repetition:
a later one (Ex. 23 c) has the curtain placed low,
but there is no repetition: the final reading (Ex. 23 d)
has both, and the repetition is strengthened by a
sequence.

23a. N. II. p. 84.

23b. N. II. p. 85.

23c. N. II. p. 85.

23d. Op. 59. II.

Presto.

The development of the scherzo melody of Op. 106 is also important for our consideration later on. We see here (Exs. 24 a and b) how the sequences, originally of two bars, become changed into one-bar sequences; and the numerous attempts to alter the up-beat (Ex. 24 c) aim at accentuating the apex.

24a. N. II. p. 130.
Allegro.

24b. Op. 106.
Assai vivace.

24c. N. II. p. 130.
meilleur
&c.

The unusual inversion of the melody in the finale of the trio Op. I. II seems to me most simply explained as an attempt to avoid the early apex.

25. N. II. p. 23.
&c.

Trio Op. I. II.
Presto.

In view of this example, I consider the statement justified that the melodic climax, when it occurs early, is often led up to by short sequences.

Undoubtedly energy radiates from a melodic apex; but the apex must be given opportunity to take full

20

effect. The progress from the sketches to the final form shows a twofold aim: firstly, to raise the apex definitely above the adjacent notes, not to give it out just before or just after these. The case of the eighth symphony (Ex. 21) shows the separation from the up-beat of an anticipatory high note. In cases like this I shall speak of 'isolation' of the apex. But it must come where there is a marked rhythmic emphasis, i.e. in the accented part of the bar. The instance just cited will serve as the first illustration of this. Perhaps the theme for the variations in sonata Op. 109 is unique as regards the simplicity of the alteration and the splendour of its effect.

26. N. I. p. 35.

Op. 109.

The immediate repetition of the opening theme with early apex is clear. The climax of the whole melody is B natural; the sketch has this note in the most unfavourable position, in the third beat of the fourth bar, i.e. as the last note of the first half. How different is the effect in the final draft! The apex, B natural, appears at the beginning of the second half, and strengthened by a harmonic anticipation. The tempo di menuetto of the violin sonata Op. 30. III also places the most effective apex, A flat, in the first part of the bar, and puts a lower up-beat before it.

Two sketches and the final reading of the third movement of the fifth symphony are distinguished from one another solely by the position given to the group forming the apex.

With reference to the second of these sketches, Nottebohm remarks: 'The pulse which the theme with its rhythmic tendency to a two-bar structure requires is more impressive just at the entry than would appear in print.' The opening bars, which doubtless were at first conceived merely as a curtain, hold the main interest and force back the apical group. This actually falls (if we think of it as in double bars) on the fourth bar, which has but little rhythmic stress. That was the reason for the removal of the opening bars: the shortening of the C is less important, and indeed does not occur in the repetition after the trio. It was not that the curtain was 'superfluous ballast', but that it masked the effect of the apex. In the other sketch, the opposite experiment was made. The apex appears without a real up-beat, in the unaccented part of the bar (double-bars); and coming so early in the theme, it is much too short to be effective in this quick tempo, unless there is repetition. The final reading avoids both these mistakes. The idea of double bars is not so compelling, the group forming the apex is lengthened, and is prepared by an ascent. It would be difficult to find a better demonstration of the importance Beethoven attached to the position of the melodic apex. Without discussing them, I shall add a few simpler and less important examples, illustrating how, even in these, the same principle holds good.

The apex may be isolated and brought out in several ways. Ex. 31 shows how, as compared with sketch a, the final form b lengthens the chief note of the apex. From sketch c we may possibly conclude that here Beethoven intended to devote the accented first part of the bar to the apex: in any case, the disposition within the bar-lines is not quite uniform. The final reading, b, syncopates the lengthened apex over the first bar-line. In another instance I have shown that, in certain circumstances, this kind of tension produces a greater stress.[1]

31 a. N. II. p. 83.

31 b. Op. 59. II.

31 c. N. II. p. 83.

In another group of alterations the apex is isolated by very long leaps, occurring either immediately before or immediately after it. This type figured very prominently in Naumann's study. The scherzo melody of the violin sonata Op. 96 shows this treatment in the seventh and eighth bars.

[1] P. Mies, 'Goethes Harfenspielgesang "Wer sich der Einsamkeit ergibt" in den Kompositionen Schuberts, Schumanns und H. Wolfs', *Zeitschrift für Aesthetik und allgemeine Kunstwissenschaft*, Bd. XVI, p. 384.

Op. 96.

The cavatina of the quartet Op. 130 was evolved exactly in the same way: the apex, set gradually higher and higher—C, E flat, F—is made more and more obvious by the drop that follows. The beginning of the quartet Op. 131 shows the same thing, as well as the addition of the up-beat (Ex. 10).

33. N. II. p. 4.

&c.   &c.

Op. 130.

Finally, the apex may be isolated by adjacent notes in unaccented parts being shortened or removed, so that their effect is diminished or eliminated. The following contrast shows this clearly: the high notes E, F, which at first interfered with the apex, are abbreviated in its favour.

34. N. I. p. 2.

Op. 49. II.

The theme of the scherzo in the cello sonata Op. 69 is a very instructive instance. The first sketch (Ex. 35 a)

25

has, it is true, an isolated apex; but the complete parallelism of the four-bar segments is disturbing.

35 a. N. II. p. 534.

35 b. N. II. p. 534.
Scherzo.

35 c. Op. 69.
Allegro molto.

The second sketch (Ex. 35 b) improves this; but now the descent from the apex is impeded. The final reading does away with this fault, and sets the second cadence in sharp contrast with the first. Becking, in his remarkable study (p. 137), has discussed the importance of this change for the scherzo character of the theme.

In the sketch (Ex. 36 a) for the quartet Op. 74 the melodic line ascends in both the half-periods; in the final reading this is changed to a consistent ascent to the apex in the middle of the melody, and a descent therefrom.

36 a. N. II. p. 93.
Presto.

36 b. Op. 74.

This form may be represented diagrammatically thus
／＼ and so is reminiscent of the typical classical
fugue theme.[1] But though Naumann[2] has shown that
the converse form (beginning with a descent) is almost
unknown in the classical fugue theme, it is to be found
in Beethoven: I have already given instances of it.
In addition to the peculiarities of these themes, with
apex at the beginning (lower up-beat, sequence, or repetition), there is often yet another; towards the end of
the theme is introduced a second apex, which balances
the first, and the way for which is carefully prepared by
sequences or special ascending forms. The diagram-
matic construction would be the reverse of the one
in the sketch, namely ＼／. It is very characteristic
of Beethoven that, at the same time, the first apex is
often prepared for in like manner. The melody of the
minuet in Op. 18. v shows this very beautifully:

37. N. II. p. 490.

Op. 18. v
Menuetto.

1st Apex.

2nd Apex.

[1] Naumann, op. cit., pp. 13, 17.
[2] Op. cit., p. 44.

27

Here a three-fold sequence introduces the apex, B natural. Jalowetz (p. 472) makes the statement: 'It is also characteristic of the technique employed by Beethoven to get melodic intensity that at the close of a piece he repeats a theme exactly, up to a certain point; but then, where in the first form of the theme the melodic line began to descend, he now adds another apex, and it is only after this that the melodic line finally declines.' This development has already been traced here in the first arrangement of the theme: the sketch still shows the normal melodic form; the final reading creates a balance between the apices. The theme of the andante cantabile in the quintet Op. 16 shows a similar transformation in the second part. The second apex D in the sketch, which, in spite of sequences, is unjustified, is finally attained by a melodic line preceding it.

38. N. II. p. 513.

Op. 16.

Whereas the transformation of the first half of the scherzo theme in Op. 106 (Ex. 24) enhances the sequence, the purpose of the second part is to bring in the second apex steadily and smoothly. As the next example, let us put side by side the beginning of the violin sonata Op. 24 from a sketch and in the final form: they require no further discussion.

From the foregoing instances, I think we may confidently conclude that Beethoven seldom placed an apex at the beginning of the theme, and considered that apices always required special introduction and special treatment; a survey of his completed works confirms the inferences drawn from the sketches. And at this point we must make a further inquiry—i.e. how far, in these style determinants, it is a question of peculiarities of Beethoven's own, and to what extent he shares them with other composers. To follow out this inquiry in detail is beyond the scope of the present book. When Gal (p. 68), comparing similar themes by Mozart and Beethoven, shows that Mozart set contrasting parts side by side, whereas Beethoven used sequences even in the construction of the melody, we may conclude that in Mozart it is rare to find the initial apex led up to by a sequence. A survey of Brahms' early pianoforte works (Op. 1–5) shows, for instance, that, unlike Beethoven, he wrote a large number of melodies that descend from the beginning, without up-

29

beat or sequence, and have a very different structure. The theme of the andante in the quintet Op. 16 (Ex. 38) resembles in character the andante theme of Brahms' piano sonata Op. 5; here also there is an apex at the beginning, but it is quite differently constructed from Beethoven's.

40. J. Brahms. Op. 5.
Andante espressivo.

In many of the foregoing points concerning the melodic apex, I consider that unquestionably we have to do with characteristic features of Beethoven's style; for they must have had vital influence on the expressive force and the effective distribution of stress. My short remarks are intended to strengthen this view, at any rate to some extent.

In my study of the songs of Brahms [1] I have shown that the melodic forms which, as their name 'ornament' suggests, have often been understood as mere external decorations of the melody, fulfil important functions in expression. Here we were able to draw from the idioms employed in the vocal music conclusions as to the instrumental music. In the present study this possibility is, of course, very limited. But once our attention is turned to the melodic apex and the way in which it is brought out, it is natural to investigate special cases, such as that from Op. 109 (Ex. 26); we pointed out how the apex is emphasized there by means of the arpeggiated chord. Thus Nottebohm was wrong in describing as 'ornament' an important note in the theme of the Waldstein Sonata Op. 53. I refer to the grace-

[1] Op. cit., p. 177 et seq.

note, C sharp, in the fourth bar, a note which is not present in the sketch (N. 80, p. 59).

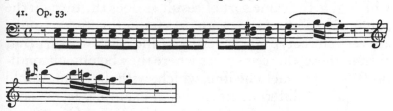

41. Op. 53.

The real explanation is simpler, but less superficial. The first apex, G, in the third bar, is steadily prepared for by the progression E—F sharp; the following bar, a sort of repetition, has nothing to set against this but the higher pitch. Here the grace-note serves to strengthen the apex; if it appears only in the final draft, it does so not as mere ornament, but in order to give more emphasis. It is not difficult to show that turns and similar elements, whether written out in full or not, have merely the purpose of emphasizing the climaxes and apices. On pp. 70 and 88 Gal gives us information about elements of this sort. But I cannot support him unconditionally when he says, referring to the beginning of the trio in Op. 1. III: 'That the turn at the beginning is purely ornamental is obvious from the fact that the string in-

42. Op. 1. III.
Allegro con brio.

struments playing in unison with the piano do not have it in their parts.' To my way of thinking, there are quite different reasons for this. Whoever has played the similar opening of the clarinet trio by Mozart (K.V. 498) must have noticed how difficult it is for the instrumentalists to execute this figure simultaneously, in spite of its being in strict rhythm. Moreover, the string

31

instruments have at their disposal certain dynamic effects, such as crescendo and vibrato on the note, which give the same sort of result as does the turn on the piano. No doubt Gal is right in saying that these figures are very stereotyped, especially in the early works. But, even in these, there are cases where they belong unconditionally to the melodic line, which, without them, would have quite a different effect: as an example, let us consider the first theme of the C minor quartet Op. 18. IV.

43. Op. 18. IV, after Joachim-Moser.

In bars 1 and 3 we have to do with a subdual of the thirds C→E flat, F→A flat, which allows the short, transient apices E flat and A flat to be emphasized. The writing of the theme for the violin in the Joachim-Moser edition shows how the player, by means of changes of position, introduces in the fifth and sixth bars the same sort of effect by means of the leaps F→D, B→F. I quote here two more examples from the early works: (1) a simple one from Op. 13, where the grace-notes in the fifth and sixth bars help to raise the line, A flat→G, of the highest notes:

44. Op. 13.

(2) In the theme from Op. 2. III (Ex. 45) the turn in the first bar is meant to correspond to the ascents C→F sharp, B→A flat:

32

45. Op. 2. III.

&c.

To get this effect, the melodic ascent in seconds in the first bar would not be sufficient. In the later works Beethoven succeeded in making this preparation with greater variety and force. The beautiful line in bars 20–21 of the cavatina in Op. 130 has the same basis, but the figure is rhythmically matched to that of the first bar.

46. Op. 130.

The grace-note at the beginning of Op. 135 seems merely to prepare the initial apex.

47. Op. 135.
Allegretto.

And the trill in the up-beat in the main theme of the sonata Op. 96 has the same force.

48. Op. 96.

The repetition of the motive in the last two examples confirms what has already been said. In all these cases, and in innumerable others, we really cannot speak of ornament. Strengthening the expressive effect of melodic apices is a peculiarity of Beethoven's manner; in the early works it is associated more or less with a structural feature in the style; later on, it becomes more complicated and forceful. Schmitz (p. 73) has also emphasized the importance of the turn as motive in Op. 18. 1.

Of interest are some cases in which the original melodies, shaped in accordance with the above instrumental principles, are altered in the vocal works to suit new expressive requirements. We shall consider this more fully in a later section. The fragment of an early opera contains the germ of the great duet in the 'Leonore'. Ex. 49 a gives the beginning of the episodic phrase:

The initial high note involves the repetition. Ex. 49 b shows the corresponding part in the sketches for the 'Leonore', with the same structural form.

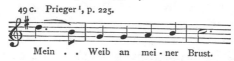

This descending formation in sequences was found inadequate to express the joy of the husband and wife at their reunion; the melody, constructed on instrumental lines, was altered to correspond closely with the feeling of the words (Ex. 49 c).

A similar thing appears in the sketches for the entrance of Pizarro:

¹ See list of abbreviations.

50c. Leonore (Prieger, p. 159).

Noch im - - mer zau - dert ihr? noch im - mer seid ihr hier, noch im - mer, noch im - mer?

The sketches show the instrumental sequences clearly; they consistently contradict the feeling of the passage. Nottebohm is right in considering them suitable for a 'jackass'. How different is the 'Leonore'! It is true that an apex like this at the beginning would be almost impossible in Beethoven's instrumental music; and here there is actually a second one, well prepared, which in some degree supports the first. Such passages show how attentively Beethoven allowed the feeling of the text to influence him, and how he tried to follow it, sometimes against his own usual practice.

(c) Repetition of notes.

In the first section I have already adduced a number of instances in which, by alteration, Beethoven avoided repetition of notes in the melodic line. Such repetition tends to bring about a sort of melodic stagnation. Many of Haydn's themes, with their gay and naïve melody, have, as Gal (p. 85) has pointed out, a tendency to repetition of notes which comes direct from folk-song. 'In thematic construction of this sort, the undeniable melodic weakness is balanced by rhythmic vivacity. The mature Beethoven, striving to make his musical idea as concentrated as possible, was naturally obliged to discard this technique, just as he was obliged to discard the mannerisms of Mozart's style. In the youthful Beethoven, the latter are to be found chiefly in the cantabile passages, to which Haydn's technique, as we have already seen, would scarcely have been applicable.'

Accordingly it would be of great interest to find instances in which the one mode of expression is converted into the other. There actually are passages of the kind, among them the following unused draft with alternative:

51. Sketches.[1]

Variant.

The alternatives come in at the places where there are conspicuous repetitions of notes. How much better the final reading with its harmonized suspension fits in with the character of the remainder of the melodic structure than does the fourfold note-repetition of the sketch!

52. Op. 59. 1.

Adagio molto e mesto.

N. II. p. 82.

[1] Veröffentlichungen des Beethovenhauses Bonn. III. 1924. *Beethoven, Unbekannte Skizzen und Entwürfe*, p. vi.

The opening theme of Sonata Op. 24 given in Ex. 39 likewise substitutes suspension for the repeated note in bar 9 (cf. Exs. 53 and 39b).

53. N. II. p. 233.

By this means the flowing melodic structure of the other bars is continued in an even stream, which undoubtedly has contributed to the name 'Spring Sonata' (Thayer, ii, p. 247). And the bars, already referred to, in the rondo of Op. 22 (Ex. 3) become more soft and flowing through the introduction of suspension; progressions are formed.

In other places progressions without suspension are substituted for repetition of notes. Compare the 'soaring' continuation of the theme in the quartet Op. 18. v:

54. N. II. p. 489.

Op. 18. v.
Allegro.

with the curious stagnation of the sketch, or the altered up-beats in the sonata Op. 90 (Ex. 1), and in the second part of the song-cycle (Ex. 2). The example from Op. 90 also shows how the rest is filled in by a repetition of notes. Even this is not mere chance: in a later section (Chapter II *g*) I shall explain it as one of the determinants of Beethoven's style, employed to produce a quite definite effect. Gal's remark about the 'naïve gaiety', like that of a folk-song, produced by note-repetition, would apply especially to the sketch for the G major quartet Op. 18. ii (Ex. 55 a):

55 a. N. ii. p. 487.

By rhythmic-harmonic enlivenment and slurring something quite different is produced (Ex. 55 b).

55 b. Op. 18. ii.
Allegro.

The sketch could never have given rise to the name 'Compliment Quartet';[1] for this demands something graceful and gallant rather than naïve—'the idea of the festive opening of some reception-hall (in the rococo period, of course), and the ceremonious presentations and reverences that follow'.

The last examples are peculiarly fitted to show how limited in their scope alterations in the melodic struc-

[1] Th. Helm, *Beethoven's Streichquartette*, p. 12.

ture often are, and how great the change in feeling associated with them may be. And we see that the element producing naïve gaiety is repetition of notes; whereas elegance and grace, such as cantabile passages especially require, are effected by suspension. This has often been pointed out before, of course; but seldom has an opportunity offered to see so clearly how the feeling underlying the whole intention seizes on unsuitable portions of the melody, and proceeds to reject, alter, and unify them.

(d) Suspension: absolute melodic structure.

In dealing with another peculiarity of Beethoven's style I can be brief—partly because I have already said something about it in the preceding pages, and partly because Gal has studied it in detail. I refer to Beethoven's treatment of suspension. On this subject Gal (p. 60) says, 'No melodic notes foreign to the chord are used except regular changing notes and diatonic passing notes in the unaccented part of the bar. Suspension is excluded, and so is chromatic progression.' Gal gives a beautiful example from a sketch for the slow movement of the fifth symphony. He calls this 'absolute melody', and defines it (p. 61) as 'a purely diatonically conceived melody, containing neither suspension nor passing notes on the accented part of the bar'. In the works of Beethoven's mature years this is the rule; it is the goal towards which the master, even while he was still young, slowly and surely strove. In the sketches there are few instances showing, as clearly as occurs in the fifth symphony, the rejection of suspension. Here we have to do with an idiosyncrasy so characteristic of Beethoven's development that eventually it seldom became necessary to make any such change. The sketches for the funeral march in the Eroica contain a very fine example. Ex. 56 shows the changes in the sixth and eighth bars:

Finally, in the eighth bar the suspension is entirely rejected: in the sixth bar there is a change in rhythm and especially in the harmonization. Gal has shown the same thing, and remarks (p. 80), 'In this way notes originally suspended become independent harmony notes, and gain proportionately in expressive force.' In the example from Op. 59. 1 (Ex. 52) I have already drawn attention to the same thing. The almost ethereal effect due to the absence of suspension is shown in a couple of bars from the adagio in Op. 106. Ex. 57 a reproduces the sketch, as follows:

57 a. N. II. p. 135.

57 b gives the completed work:

57 b. Op. 106.

These chords without suspension appear in admirable contrast to the crowded ones in the preceding bars —a triumph of 'absolute melody'.

Naturally those instances are of interest to us where,

in contrast to the foregoing, suspensions are afterwards introduced. As a matter of fact, this happens more frequently; but the instances can be brought together in a few groups and arranged under certain effects. Thus in Chapter I *c* I have already mentioned the substitution of suspension for repetition of notes (Exs. 3, 53) in order to produce a flowing effect. A second group has its origin in an endeavour to meet the requirements of form. Here, as in cases previously adduced, up-beats are added so as to correspond to up-beats occurring later. The minuet in sonata Op. 10. III illustrates this in the sketch and the final reading of bars 7–8: originally only the last bar of the melody had the suspension. The result is a sort of musical rhyme.

58. N. II. p. 39.

Op. 10. III.

Menuetto.

And to this group belongs the development of the alla danza tedesca from Op. 130. A sketch in A major of the movement—

41

was originally intended for the A minor quartet Op. 132: neither in the fourth nor in the eighth bar has it the suspension it receives in the final reading; only the second and third quavers in the eighth bar of the sketch contain something of the kind.

59 b. Op. 130.
Alla danza tedesca. Allegro assai.

In a further sketch (Ex. 59 c) this flowing line has become a suspension—indeed, as the final form shows, a fully harmonized one.

The fourth bar is missing, as if Beethoven were not quite clear about it. A later sketch (Ex. 59 d) in B flat major has the suspension in bar 4 also, but resting on bar 3. It is only in the final reading, however, that one gets the complete suspension in one bar independently.

59 d.   N. II. p. 3.
Allemande. Allegro.

The flowing line, then, was the basic idea. At first it developed into the fully harmonized suspension in bar 3; then for a time it was not so clear. And this involved the suspension in bar 4, for the sake of symmetry. What Gal has demonstrated is not affected by these examples; in all of them the idea leading to the suspension is perfectly obvious.

Twice already I have mentioned groups of alterations that have come about in obedience to principles governing form. And for an understanding of the development of the melodic form comparison of the sketches and the finished works yields valuable information.

II

THE MELODIC FORM

(a) The types of melody.

W. FISCHER has made some important contributions to
the study of form in the classics. In what follows I propose to assume and make use of the ideas he has advanced; so it may be as well to set them forth here
briefly in his own words. He distinguishes two types
of melody—the song type (S-type) and the continuation
type (C-type). Concerning the former, he says (p. 26):
'The antecedent of the period is a group of two phrases
(α and β); in the subsequent these are repeated in their
entirety, either unaltered or with modification of the
second part (β). In every case α reappears note for
note.' (Ex. 60.)

60. J. S. Bach. Rondeau. Fischer, p. 26.

And concerning the C-type (p. 29): 'After an antecedent with perfect or imperfect cadence, there follows
a modulating "continuation", where materials may or
may not be related to what precedes it, and which consists of one or more consecutive sequences; frequently
a third group acts as a "conclusion" or "epilogue" to the
whole'. According to Fischer, Ex. 61 illustrates this
type 'in its highest perfection'.

44

A + b constitutes the antecedent, c is the continuation with sequences, d is the conclusion. Fischer goes on to state (p. 62): 'In the neo-classical style, melodies, either of the S-type or closely allied to it as regards their form, are fitted into the frame provided by the baroque C-type.' Or, somewhat differently expressed (p. 52): 'The C-type develops into the form of exposition of the

45

sonata movement, with exclusion, of course, of the second section.' Fischer (p. 51) instances a theme by Pergolesi as an example of the transition, 'where the first subject of a melody framed on the C-type is constructed on the S-type'. Space will not admit of my dealing further with the matter here; I shall discuss the importance of these sections more fully in a later part of the book.

The definition of the two types of melody shows that repetitions and sequences fulfil an important rôle. And in Chapter I we have already dealt with these structures. So let us now consider the groups of alterations and those cases which have to do with the formation and arrangement of repetitions and sequences.

(b) Threefold repetition.

Gal (p. 68) has shown how, in the episodic theme of the 'Coriolanus' overture, a four-bar group is formed by threefold repetition, and he has drawn attention to the logical way in which this is introduced. Later (pp. 111–12) he adduces similar instances of groups used in the working-out. As a matter of fact, it is possible to demonstrate this threefold repetition everywhere throughout the structure both of theme and of movement, and in their larger as well as in their more detailed aspects. Before I proceed to this systematically, I should like to show, in one developmental series, how Beethoven arrived at the formation of themes of this kind. Nottebohm gives a series of sketches for the first theme of the quartet Op. 18. 1; let me reproduce some of these, together with the final reading.

62 a.   N. II. p. 481.   (?)

62 b contains a threefold repetition, but it is very 'short-winded'.

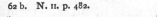

62 c reverts to a sort of S-type with a fourfold repetition of the first motive.

62 c. N. II. p. 482.

After much experimenting, the final form shows the threefold repetition of the opening motive with the construction $1 : 2 : 1 + 2 + 2^1$, in which, however, the third two-bar group is an intensified repetition of the first two.

62 d. Op. 18. I.

Allegro con brio.

It is not very easy to decide as to which type of melody this finally belongs. There can be no question of an eight-bar S-type, for the second two bars in no way correspond to the fourth two. The continuation (see Ex. 109) suggests that we have here an eight-bar antecedent of a C-type. There are many other instances of the kind. The scherzo of Sonata Op. 14. II shows threefold repetition of the same short motive.

63. Op. 14. II. Scherzo.

Allegro assai.

---

¹ See list of abbreviations.

47

In other respects this is a clear case of an S 8-type.[1]
It is obvious that a melodic structure of this kind must
affect the whole movement; and, as a matter of fact, the
threefold repetition reappears again and again. A similar example is the theme of the finale in Op. 10. 1; here
also we have to do with an S 8.

64. Op. 10. 1.
Prestissimo.

But this is not true of the second theme in the same
movement; this consists of two motives in two-bar structure, each of which is repeated three times, though with
changes of form.

65. Op. 10. 1.

Two-bar motives of this kind arranged in threefold
sequence appear also in the theme of Sonata Op. 2. 11;
when it comes in for the third time, the motive is reduced to its elementary form and then carried on.

[1] See list of abbreviations.

66. Op. 2. II.

This gives a C 8 with the structure $2 \times 2 + 4 \times 1$, and

underbraces: anteced. contin.

having the motives of the sequences connected one with the other. The second theme of the same movement shows a threefold repetition of motives written in four and in six bars.

67. Op. 2. II.

This gives a C-type with the structure $2 \times 4 + 3$

$+ 3 \times 2 + 1$. Among many other examples I shall mention only the trio in Op. 10. II.

68. Op. 10. II.

49

The structure in this is clearly $3 \times 4 + 4$; accordingly, it can scarcely be regarded as an S, but rather as a special case of a C 16. The same melodic structure that we find in the antecedents of the first and second themes also appears in the episodic sections and in the subsequents; likewise, in the consequent in Sonata Op. 7, we get the consequent of a C 12:

69 a. Op. 7.

and in that in the Sonata Op. 106 the consequent of a C 8:

69 b. Op. 106.

Gal pointed this out (p. 113); and he makes it very clear from the instances he gives. 'In his mature years Beethoven feels this threefold repetition to be redundant.' If this remark of Gal's is true of the threefold repetitions in the working-out, it also holds good of the thematic construction. In the compositions up to Op. 30–31 such repetitions are very common; after that they occur only now and then, and in an especially happy form. We find them, for instance, in the theme of Op. 106 (Ex. 69) and in the theme for variations in Op. 109 (Ex. 26); or again, in scherzi and similar movements, such as the presto in Op. 130, where we have an S 8 with the structure $\underbrace{3 \times 1 + 1}_{a} + \underbrace{3 \times 1 + 1}_{a}$, or in the scherzando in Op. 127, where the form is the same; in the presto in Op. 74 we get a C 8 running thus: $\underbrace{3 \times 1 + 1}_{a} + \underbrace{3 \times 1 + 1}_{\beta}$ (Ex. 36); the sketch makes the original intention still clearer.

This melodic structure has certain disadvantages; it produces clear-cut caesurae at every two bars, which become inconspicuous only when the tempo gets rapid. In his early work Beethoven was satisfied with this structure; later on he used it only where it could do no harm. In the threefold repetition in thematic structure we have one of the stylistic features characteristic of Beethoven as a young man.

We learn something more, however, from these considerations. The S-type is usually in eight bars, and, so to speak, square; this follows inevitably from its origin in folk-song and dance tunes (Fischer, p. 29). But in Beethoven the C-types of melody also have the same number of bars.[1] This would seem to justify Ricmann's theory that every melody is constructed in the form [2]:

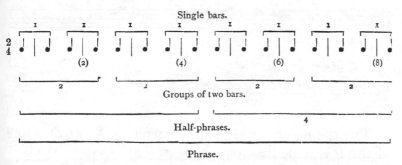

the rule being 'that the continued contrasting of units of the same magnitude, the first answered by a

[1] See Chap. II *f*.
[2] *System der musikalischen Rhythmik und Metrik,* p. 198.

second of the same order, builds the foundation of the structure of musical form'. In Exs. 62d, 68, and 69b there can be no question of this. The *last* part is set in contrast to the *three* first, which just suffice to balance it in spite of the greater number of bars they contain; conversely, the last part, in spite of its brevity, is able to intensify the effect through its very unlikeness, both rhythmical and melodic, to the other two. How the regular C-type is arrived at in the case of Beethoven's music will become still clearer as we proceed; it is already obvious that its structure is quite different from the S-type: 'the first subject is not answered by a second subject of the same order.' Sondheimer's [1] 'proof that a square dance-rhythm is not the basis of modern instrumental music' seems to me to find support in the case of Beethoven through our discovery of this principle in his thematic construction.

Where else do we find melodic construction with threefold repetition of the motive? Mozart uses it very seldom, and then usually in episodic sections and in unimportant passages, such as occur, for instance, in the pianoforte sonata in C major (K.V. 309).

70. KV. 309.

The theme of the C major quartet (K.V. 465) is one of the few melodies that show it.

KV. 465.

[1] *Zeitschr. f. Musikwiss.*, III. Jahrg., p. 87.

In Haydn's music it is still rarer. Jalowetz, however, has pointed out the relation between the melody in Beethoven's early music and that of Philipp Emanuel Bach; and he has picked out a theme by that composer as counter-theme to the last section of Op. 7 (pp. 457–8). And this theme of Ph. E. Bach shows clearly what is far less obvious in Beethoven, i.e. the threefold repetition.

71. Beethoven, Op. 7.

Ph. E. Bach. Jalowetz, p. 458.

As a matter of fact, this structure appears throughout all Philipp Emanuel Bach's 'Sonaten für Kenner und Liebhaber'. It also occurs in the final allegro of sonata I, in rondo II (Ex. 78) in the second collection, in the first allegro and in the allegro di molto of sonata I, and in the allegro assai of sonata III—all of which are in the third collection; many other instances are to be found in the other collections. Here therefore we have a new feature common to both artists, over and above the one pointed out by Jalowetz and Oppel.[1] For I consider that we are not dealing here with a conscious dependence of one artist on another; and an unconscious transference

[1] D. R. Oppel, 'Über Beziehungen Beethovens zu Mozart und zu Ph. E. Bach,' *Zeitschr. f. Musikwiss.*, Jahrg. V.

of formal features of this sort is explicable only when there is common ground in the character of the music itself. I consider this condition very well exemplified in the case of these two artists.

As we have seen, threefold repetition served for construction of the theme; there are other cases where it is employed to build up a movement or a part of a movement. Gal goes so far as to interpret these threefold groups in the working-out as an attempt to 'expand the form' (p. 113). In simple song-melodies we constantly find the threefold repetitions of a phrase, and especially of its first half; in the same way, it is very common to find a whole melody repeated three times in slow movements and in rondos. An instance of this occurs in the third movement of the serenade Op. 8, where two melodies—adagio—allegro molto—adagio—allegro molto—adagio—appear alternatively; and the slow movement of the violin sonata Op. 30. 1 brings in the main theme three times. This can scarcely be regarded as a peculiarity of Beethoven's.

It is another matter altogether when we proceed to follow out the development of this idea in cases where the form has to be expanded in movements of minuet or scherzo character occurring in the works between Op. 70 and Op. 100 roughly. Here we have not so much a special feature of the scherzo, in Becking's sense, as a middle section. We find a transition to this in the scherzo of the pianoforte trio Op. 97. The first part of the scherzo theme consists of $16 = 2 \times 8$ bars; then follows the second part; and to this is immediately appended the melody of the trio plus the first part. The repetition-signs show that all this is to be played twice; then follows the second part of the scherzo, and after that comes the coda, which gives us the following structure:

Part I ‖ : Part II Trio Part I : ‖ Part II Coda

Scherzo

and this means that the scherzo melody occurs three times. This form occurs in full in the presto of Op. 74, in the presto of the seventh symphony, Op. 92, in the trio portion of the allegro assai vivace ma serioso in Op. 95 (though with fundamental changes), and then finally in the presto of Op. 131. There have always been minuets and other dance-forms with two alternating passages in which the main melody is repeated three times. But to expand this form with an episode is undoubtedly one of Beethoven's peculiarities as a composer; and even in his work it occurs only for a relatively short period. Later on, Schumann revived it in some degree, when, as in the second symphony, the pianoforte quintet and the third pianoforte trio, he expanded the several parts; but he made a departure by introducing two trios. This is an instance of the way in which a composer of the romantic school dealt with and modified the development introduced by Beethoven; in Beethoven's own work the form is expanded, but the thematic material remains unaltered; in Schumann the material is expanded, and it is the form that remains unaltered. Later on, as in the molto vivace of the ninth symphony, we get, however, some expansion of the theme, in which fugato plays an important part.

In his earlier work Beethoven effected this expansion in other ways, as can be seen by comparing the octet for wind-instruments Op. 103 with the string quintet Op. 4. Altmann [1] has pointed out that the quintet is not a mere re-instrumentation of the octet, but has been rewritten and expanded from first to last. The final movement of 223 bars in the octet, for instance, is extended in the quintet to 418 bars. This movement can be divided up into some four sections. In the following table the comparison is brought out:

[1] W. Altmann, 'Beethovens Streichquintett Op. 4. 1. *Beethovenheft der Musik*', 1902, p. 1097. Cf. A. Orel, 'Beethovens Oktett Op. 103 und seine Bearbeitung als Quintett Op. 4', *Zeitschr. f. Musikwissensch.*, Jahrg. III.

	Op. 4.	Op. 103.	Difference.
(a) The first theme with its working-out and repetition	164	90	74
(b) The middle section, up to the repetition of the first theme	72	61	11
(c) Up to the re-entry of the middle section	87	47	40
(d) The repetition of the middle section, and the coda	95	25	70
	418	223	195

The main increase, apart from the addition of the coda, concerns the development of the first theme, which is ten bars in length. The octet immediately starts a thematic elaboration, and, after introducing a little bridge-motive in the fifty-seventh bar, repeats the theme. The quintet has an eight-bar episode after the ten-bar theme, and then immediately repeats the theme. In this way the 'complex' of the first theme is given the form $10+8+10$, and runs to 28 bars. As a natural consequence, all the parts connected with it share in the expansion. After the 28 bars of the theme there follows the thematic working-out, as far as bar 97; and then the whole theme begins again. Finally it becomes obvious that the coda must be expanded, since it is derived from the theme. We can see here what a variety of experiments Beethoven made in order to bring about successfully an expansion of form.

(c) *Avoidance of sequences and uniform rhythms; characteristic relations between the melodic types, and their changes.*

Writers have frequently laid stress on the importance of sequences in the formation of Beethoven's themes and elaborations generally. In addition to the passages already mentioned (in a certain measure the threefold repetition also belongs to this category) I shall refer to the treatment of individual themes in the third and fifth symphonies pointed out by Schmitz (pp. 79, 84). I have already made it clear that this threefold repetition is a feature of Beethoven's early style.

There are actually instances where melodies, at first constructed on this principle, are altered so that the essential melody is retained but the repetition is avoided. The theme of the first march for four hands shows in the final reading a substitution of a sequence for the third repetition in the sketch.

72a. N. 80. p. 55.

bars 8–9.

72b. Op. 45. I.

bars 1–4.

bars 8–9.

And I may also cite here as interesting the alteration in the theme for variations from Op. 18. v (Ex. 8) already referred to. The sketch shows threefold repetition, but at the same time a marked S-type: i.e. it shows liaisons of two kinds, as is shown by the following table:

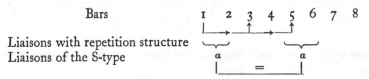

Bars	1	2	3	4	5	6	7	8
Liaisons with repetition structure								
Liaisons of the S-type								

This gives the whole thing a rhythmical and melodic monotony which is avoided in the final theme, a pure S-type.

This association of repetition and sequences in the forming of a theme is a kind of logical construction from a motive provided by the imagination. Out of such a motive the construction promptly develops a theme, which has then to be modified in consequence of its too regular rhythm or of the predominance of sequences. I propose to deal more fully later on with the psychological aspect of this process: here I shall merely give a few more examples. In Ex. 6 we saw sketches for the final theme of Op. 132; Ex. 73 shows other stages in the development to the final form; and we see in these how the uniformity of the sketches is increasingly avoided. We shall return to the question of the theme later on.

73 a. N. II. p. 466.

73 b. N. II. p. 549.

73 c. Op. 132.
Allegro appassionato.

As we may judge from the sketches, the beautiful middle section of the adagio of the ninth symphony also suffered from too great uniformity of rhythm, a fault that was soon corrected by alteration of the melody in the third bar, together with addition of an up-beat and syncopation.

At the beginning of the second part of the march Op. 45. 1 we see how a series of short sequences is avoided through rhythmical and melodic changes in the first segment as contrasted with those that follow. Among other instances of the kind may be mentioned the theme of the last movement in Op. 18. 1; in the sketch this begins with a half-bar sequence which is avoided in the final form.

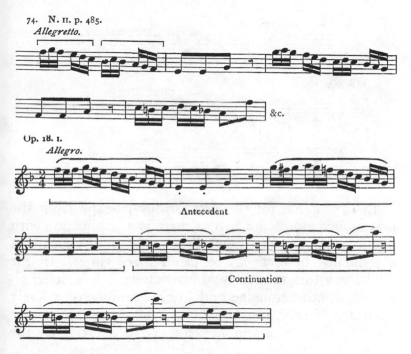

74.   N. II. p. 485.
Allegretto.

&c.

Op. 18. 1.
Allegro.

Antecedent

Continuation

In this example we see a number of things to which I have already drawn attention. In the sketch, the highest point of the first motive lies in a very unfavourable place; but in the final reading this is rectified. The apex of the theme comes early, so a repetition immediately follows; bar 7 contains a second apex, the way for which is carefully prepared. The continuation (we are

59

dealing here with a C 8) is formed by threefold repetition. It is possible that the fifth bar in the sketch suggested the alteration. We should also consider here the scherzo theme of the cello sonata Op. 69 (Ex. 35), where the threefold repetition is deliberately avoided.

Finally, let me mention certain cases which do not concern the theme but other 'complexes'. The end of the first part of the bagatelle Op. 126. II was sketched out by Beethoven as we see it in Ex. 75 a: and our admiration must be roused by the skill with which he avoids the sequences in the final reading Ex. 75 b.

In the sketch for the first bridge-passage from the first movement of the Eroica there is a triplication with a repetition of notes; then follows an ascent by means of a sequence in seconds, repeated three times. In the final form this is greatly abbreviated; it is written almost without sequence and in the manner of a lively up-beat. Finally, there is the instance, already cited in Ex. 16, where the simple sequence is masked by the aid of lively up-beats formed in various ways.

Third Symphony.

In other groups showing alteration of the structure of the sequences we see the development of perfectly definite types of melody.

The essential feature in these types lies in the relations between the several parts of the melody. The example on p. 47 shows what these are. The way in which they are grouped is characteristic of each type. In the S-type they follow in successive groups, the second linked to the first (H. Riemann); isolated parts of the melody, such as bars 1–2 and 5–6, are alike, both as regards motive and rhythm (Ex. 60). The C-type is different; the successive parts are connected by virtue of sequences and repetitions. Fischer has shown that 'where the antecedent is made up of a number of segments, the motives of the sequences in the continuation are always shorter; as soon as the continuation begins, we get a contraction of the rhythm'. In what follows I shall refer to this phenomenon as 'sequence-contraction'. I consider that what is essential in shaping the form is to order the relations of the final melody in such a way that they suffice to unify it and make it hold together; but they must not be so numerous that the independence of the several parts is seriously imperilled: for this leads to the form's becoming unrecognizable. Ex. 8 illustrates this. It is possible to find in the sketches a number of groups in which we can see a unified type of melody develop out of a condition in which there was a superfluity of liaisons consisting of sequences and regular rhythms. The theme from Op. 132 (Exs. 6 and 73), to which I have already referred so frequently, belongs here. From the first drafts it is not possible to ascribe it to any particular type of melody, either on account of, or in spite of, the rhythmic liaisons between bar and bar (Ex. 6); it has a certain unity, but is not well put together. In its second stage (which, however, may possibly not

61

belong to this developmental series) it is a C-type; there is a four-bar antecedent with two-bar liaisons, and at the end we find a sequence-contraction. The next sketch (Ex. 73 b) has none of these organizing liaisons; it is to be regarded merely as an eight-bar antecedent of a C-type which also has a course of eight bars. In the final form (Ex. 73 c), which is distinguished from the others by something additional (see Chapter II g), liaisons are again established between bars 1, 3 and 6 by means of similarity in the rhythmical treatment. The theme of the second movement in Op. 14.1 is badly held together in its sketched form (Ex. 77 a).

77 a. N. II. p. 55.

It begins with triplication of one bar; then follows a two-bar repetition. Obviously this is very faulty architecture. And in the final form it is changed.

77 b. Op. 14. 1.
Allegretto.

Here the repetition of the first bar is cut down, and that of the two-bar part is dropped out altogether; the theme seems to be written in half-bars, and the end-result is an indubitable S-type of 16 = 8 bars, with liaisons characteristic of that type. Just as in the previous example, this S is a sort of antecedent in a larger

C-type. The adagio theme of Op. 59. 1 had originally
only six bars, the fifth with short sequences; the order of
the liaisons was not clear.

78. N. II. p. 82.

Op. 59. 1.

Adagio molto e mesto.

Antecedent

Continuation

Out of this developed a C 8 with a four-bar antecedent and four-bar continuation; the rhythmical connexion between bars 1–2 and 5–6 is too slight for an
S. And here we see something that we shall frequently
meet with again, i.e. the birth of a regular eight-bar
theme out of one of about six bars ('irregular' in
Riemann's sense). But, as was pointed out above, its
genesis shows clearly that the structural form here is
that of an C- and not of a S-type. This form and the
same organization also appear in the episodic passages.
Ex. 79 a gives the episodic bars in the first theme of the
concerto Op. 15 as they appear in the sketch: there is an
obvious triplication, and bar 7 shows reference to bars 1,
3 and 5; but we find no development of any kind.

79 a. N. II, p. 64.

In the final form this superfluity of liaisons is avoided, and instead we get a regular S-type, in which the essential theme is preserved.

79 b. Op. 15.

The allegro theme of the Sonata Op. 101 also furnishes a beautiful instance of the way in which liaisons of this kind are changed into a C 8.

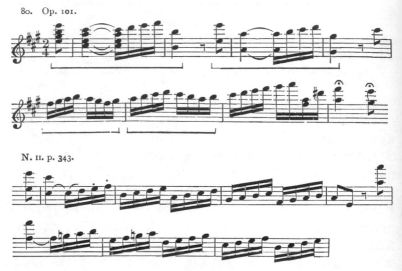

80. Op. 101.

N. II. p. 343.

The original draft is short-winded and without definite form; from it is evolved a fine example of a C 8. The antecedent has four bars with the structure 2×2; the continuation also has four bars showing sequence-contraction, $2 \times 1 + 2$. Here again we see what importance Beethoven attached to getting the form clear: for in the final solutions thematic unity is always associated with an arrangement of the liaisons that leads to greater intelligibility.

Op. 59. II and the first movement of the eighth

symphony contain two very instructive examples. In Ex. 23 I gave three sketches for the presto of this work. Ex. 23 a is an S-type that shows a very special peculiarity. Elsewhere [1] I have shown that it is not justifiable to apply the concept of 'symmetry' to the normal S-type; but here symmetry is actually produced, and might be reproduced diagrammatically somewhat as follows:

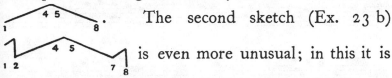 The second sketch (Ex. 23 b) is even more unusual; in this it is impossible to recognize either the S- or the C-type. And we find that Beethoven also rejected this arrangement of the liaisons. What did he substitute for it? An eight-bar C-type with a four-bar antecedent ($\| : 2 : \|$) followed by a continuation of four bars showing sequence-contraction (Ex. 81).

81. N. ii. p. 85.

It would appear that the symmetrical liaisons did not satisfy Beethoven's architectural sense; the episodic theme of the first movement in the eighth symphony seems to corroborate this impression. In the sketch for this the line to the apex is quite symmetrical. Both the antecedent and subsequent are formed by triplication; and, since the motives correspond, this makes the whole look as though it belonged to the

[1] *Zeitschrift für Musikwissenschaft.* Notice of W. Werker, 'Die Matthäus-Passion'.

S-type. In the final form the same construction is kept, but the two motives are differently fashioned, so that the curve is different on its two sides. We get more the impression of a C 8-type: which shows what a narrow line separates the two types of melody when it comes to the extreme cases.

82. N. II. p. III.

Eighth Symphony.

In the article referred to, I showed that it is possible to make music strictly symmetrical by technical means without our feeling corresponding to this in any way. The way in which these two almost symmetrical themes were altered, and the fact that really symmetrical melodies seldom, if ever, occur, seem to justify my opinion and to give it the support of a very important witness, i.e. Beethoven himself. Lorenz [1] has shown that in the arrangement of Wagner's melodies there is a plan—a, b, c, b, a—and this he calls the 'perfect curve' (a, b, and c stand for the several melodies). But the fact that a structure so simple as this has escaped detection for so long is, to my way of thinking, just so much the more proof that no acoustic or aesthetic equivalent for it exists.

In this connexion the change made in the scherzo theme of Op. 106 is instructive. It has often been observed

[1] A. Lorenz, 'Gedanken und Studien zur musikalischen Form-gebung', in R. Wagner's 'Ring des Nibelungen', pp. 60, 92.

that the melody consists of seven bars. The sketch (Ex. 24 a) is a C 8 with a beautiful sequence-contraction and the construction $2 \times 2 + 3 \times 1 + 1$. But the same

(anteced.) (contin.)

movement is also held together by liaisons which occur either between bars, by means of their common rhythmical structure , or by the ascending and descending seconds in bars 2, 4 | 5, 7. In the final form, it is true, these liaisons are cut out, the repeated motive is shortened by one bar (probably on account of the early apex) and the triplication is added. The concluding bar should really come then, but this does not appear in the original form. It was omitted, and in its place there was added a further triplication with an appropriate final bar. Becking (p. 141) has already pointed out the importance of this irregularity with regard to the scherzo character. This seven-bar melody is undoubtedly a peculiarity, and it can never be understood as an S-type, but as a C-type in conjunction with threefold repetition. An example like this shows that Beethoven was aware of the superabundance of liaisons and sequences; the quick tempo (double bars, according to Becking) makes the rhythmical structure from bar to bar less conspicuous. Similar experiments—though less successful in the final form, it is true—prepared the way for the theme for variations in the quartet Op. 74. A first sketch (Ex. 83 a) shows clearly the structure of the threefold repetition $3 \times 2 + 2$, or, where in the third the change appears too extensive, the eight-bar C-type $2 \times 2 + 2 \times 1 + 2$; here the same motive appears six times.

83 a. N. II. p. 94.

Antecedent   Continuation

In Ex. 83 b an attempt is made to improve on this by a change in bar 3, without further justification.

In the final reading the two-bar sequences are cut out. Does this not involve a loss of structural stability? It is clear that Beethoven recognized that the sequences of the original form were in some degree logical; but the construction finally adopted is not quite sure, nor quite intelligible.

83 c.   Op. 74.

Allegretto con Variazioni.

That the formation of such sequences may be essential to the musical expression is shown by the developmental stages of the melody 'In des Lebens Frühlingstagen' from 'Leonore'. The sketches in Ex. 84 make it clear that Beethoven was trying to use as much as possible descending seconds, intervals that are well known to produce a soft and sighing effect,[1] further aided here by the suspension. (See p. 36.)

84 a.   N. II. p. 420.   b.

In des Le-bens Früh-lings-ta - gen.   In des Le - bens

c.   d.

In   In

e.   f.   Prieger, p. 178.

In   In des   Le - bens Frühlings-ta - gen.

[1] P. Mies, 'Über die Tonmalerei', *Zeitschrift für Aesthetik und allgemeine Kunstwissenschaft*, Bd. VII, p. 432 et seq.

But to get shape into this involved difficulties. The first sketch (a) has still got two ascending seconds, one third, and one ground-note; sketch (b) has a ragged beginning and is without liaisons; sketch (c) has been smoothed down, but is otherwise much the same as (b). Sketch (d) is the first to contain definite sequences, but it also has an up-beat third and fourth. It is only in the following draft that Beethoven attains his object; except for one fourth, there are only descending seconds and ground-notes, and, as a consequence of the early apex, there are very beautiful sequences and repetitions. In the final form (f) the second apex is further emphasized by a grace-note, and a new descending second is introduced; by these means the intended expression is achieved. I consider that in the works of the great masters we do not find excessive divorce between form and content: nothing short of the right form will release the desired content; the expression sought will reveal itself only when the form adequate to it has been found. The two are indissolubly connected.[1]

In the foregoing paragraphs I have dealt mainly with the excision of superfluous liaisons conditioned by the rhythmic structure or by sequences. I shall now refer to some cases in which the liaisons depend on similarities in the melodic structure. It is impossible, of course, to draw a hard and fast line between these and the preceding. All I am concerned to show is that Beethoven finally selected, from out the superabundant liaisons, just those which were characteristic of the particular type of melody adopted in the final reading. And in this connexion there is an interesting case quoted by Gal (p. 94) from the second symphony, where the melodic liaison in bars 5 and 7 is weakened, so that there remain only those belonging to the S-type.

---

[1] E. Utitz comes to similar conclusions in 'Zum Schaffen des Künstlers', *Zeitschrift für Aesthetik und allgemeine Kunstwissenschaft*, Bd. XVIII, p. 67.

Second Symphony.

The theme of the trio in the eighth symphony was originally written with a threefold repetition on the plan $3 \times 2 \times 2$ (Ex. 4). The next sketch shows its transformation into an S-type, but still with the first and third bars alike: which is an unnecessary relationship. In the final reading this also is eliminated, and the consequent is given more variety. We find this latter improvement elsewhere—for instance, in the trio of the Eroica, which at first was sketched out as the simplest sort of S-type (Ex. 86).

86. N. 80. p. 48.

Third Symphony.

Antecedent   Consequent

In the theme of the last movement of the quartet Op. 18. vi the form given to the liaisons is altered very extensively. The first experiment (Ex. 87 a) makes use of threefold repetition:

87 a. N. II. p. 61.

but the result is unsatisfactory and lacks unity. The second sketch also shows the triplication, but the repetitions are linked together into an S-type; thematically, they are derived from the final motive of the first.

87 b. *Allegretto.*

In the next attempt (Ex. 87 c) a true S-type is attained, but there are even more liaisons in it.

87 c. N. II. p. 62.

The theme when finished is very important as regards its form. It is an S 16: the antecedent and consequent have different cadences, but each is a C 8. The result is a mixed type, such as we shall frequently encounter again. I propose to describe them as S (C).[1]

[1] See list of abbreviations.

Allegretto quasi Allegro.

The structure of the whole theme then is as follows:

$$2 \times 2 + 2 \times 1 + 2 + 2 \times 2 + 2 \times 1 + 2$$

anteced. contin. anteced. contin.

of C-types

Antecedent   =   Consequent

of the S-type

$$CF_7 \qquad\qquad CF_7B_6$$

cadences.

But even the first sketch foreshadows the introduction of the Malinconia theme. The above examples should suffice. We see in them clearly that Beethoven was striving after an intelligible and characteristic thematic form; but at the same time it is apparent that the completed form was not a flash of inspiration that came at the first moment, but the result of retaining a certain rhythmical and thematic structure throughout the many changes to which the work was subjected.

In settling what are the liaisons characteristic of a melodic type, we may find that the reverse process occurs: it may be found necessary to introduce liaisons that were lacking in the sketch. As a matter of fact, this happens more seldom. In the sketch (Ex. 88 a) the theme of the minuet in Op. 59. III is not of any definite type, but in the final reading (Ex. 88 c) it becomes a typical S 8.

88 a. N. II. p. 86.

88 b. N. II. p. 87.

88 c. Op. 59. III.
Menuetto, Gracioso.

The theme of the second movement of the ninth symphony was made up of two fugue themes dating from the years 1815 and 1817 (Ex. 89 a, b).

89 a. N. II. p. 157, 1815.
Fugue.

89 b. N. II. p. 158, 1817.

The beginning of a longer sketch (Ex. 89 c) shows a similar mixture:

89 c. N. II. p. 171, 1823.
Presto.

(?)

Little by little, the raggedness of the beginning is

smoothed away, the quavers disappear, and with their disappearance the melodic line becomes better unified (Ex. 89 d). From the sketch (Ex. 89 e) we may perhaps conclude that the idea of 'Ritmo di tre battute' was the germ from which this unification arose.

89 d. Ninth Symphony.

89 e. N. II. p. 172.

The theme of the second movement of the fifth symphony had to pass through the same process of transformation. Ex. 90 a gives a sketch with the superscription 'Andante quasi menuetto'.

90 a. N. I. p. 14.
Andante quasi menuetto.

The sequence is obvious; the dotted rhythm in the writing in quavers fits the minuet character. Another sketch (Ex. 90 b) shows these dotted rhythms only in the last bars, i.e. in the continuation; and, apart from the altered up-beat, the sequence seems to me less clear; the descending third, D flat—B flat, in bar 3 does not correspond so closely to the C—A flat in bar 1.

90 b. N. II. p. 534.

&c.

A further sketch (Ex. 90 c) shows that the dots were not merely forgotten.

90 c. N. I. p. 63.

&c.

In the finished work (Ex. 90 c) the dotted rhythms appear again, and in this way the descending third in bar 3 is once more brought into prominence. The result is a definite C 8 with the structure

$$\underbrace{2 \times 2}_{\text{anteced.}} + \underbrace{2 \times 1 + 2}_{\text{contin.}}$$

90 c.   Fifth Symphony.
Andante con moto.

The sketch for the minuet melody in the trio Op. 1. III is also without characteristic liaisons. In the final form the first and second bars of the sketch are cut out, and as third bar a motive is introduced that corresponds with bars 7–8 in the sketch.

91.   N. II. p. 25.

Op. 1. III.
Menuetto.
Quasi allegro.

The outcome of these changes is a regular S-type with a rest in place of the eighth bar. This S-type is the

75

antecedent of a C-type, and the whole theme has accordingly the structure of a C (S)-type,[1] with the structure

$$2+2+2+1+\frown+3\times1+3\times\tfrac{1}{3}+1$$

$$\underbrace{\overset{a\quad\beta\quad a\quad\beta}{}}_{\text{antecedent}}\underbrace{}_{\text{continuation}}$$

The adagio theme of Sonata Op. 96 is also without unity of form in the sketch. The relation between bars 5–6 and 1–2 is too slight for an S-type; conversely, the similarity between bars 5–6 and 7–8 is out of keeping, and the development necessary for a C-type is lacking.

92. N. I. p. 26.

Op. 96
Adagio espressivo.

The finished work, on the other hand, is definitely of the S-type; bars 1–2 and 5–6 are rhythmically alike, and the repetitions have dropped out.

(d) *Sequence-contractions.*

I have already pointed out (p. 61) that I agree with Fischer on the importance of sequence-contractions as a form of melodic liaison. The relation of the length of sequence in the antecedent to that in the consequent, and the working-out of the contraction, are matters of vital importance to the elasticity of the theme in the C-type. In one group of alterations, where the theme may originally be of the S-type, the characteristic feature is the development to a C 8, C 16, &c. The last

[1] See list of abbreviations.

movement of the trio Op. 97 had in the sketch (Ex.
93 a) a C 8 as its first part, with the structure
2 × 2 + 4; this was followed by an S 8 as the second
part. In a later sketch this second part has already
undergone contraction.

93 a.   N. ii. 285.

From this the final reading (Ex. 93 b) proceeds logically on the plan 3 × 1 + 3 × 1 + 2.

93 b.   Op. 97.
Allegro moderato.

The whole thing, accordingly, is a C, in which both
the antecedent and the continuation are also built on
that type. The small subsidiary half-bar sequences in
the continuation are important to the development,

which is completely lacking in the sketch, where the two types are merely set side by side. The special character of the form is in no way affected by the fact that the repetitions are varied in the two parts although the harmonization is the same. The middle portion of the funeral march in Op. 26 displays well the tensity and force which, in certain circumstances, the contracted C-type may assume.

94. N. II. p. 241.

Op. 26.

The sketch has an antecedent of four bars, which may be regarded as a sort of S-type. In the finished work this somewhat trivial regularity is replaced by a C 4 with wonderfully effective contractions. It is built as follows:

$$\underbrace{2 \times 1}_{\text{anteced.}} + \underbrace{2 \times \tfrac{1}{2} + 3 \times \tfrac{1}{4}}_{\text{contin.}} + \underbrace{\tfrac{1}{4}}_{\text{conseq.}}$$

This effect is much employed in episodic sections.

In the minuet theme of Op. 59. III, the first part of which appeared in Ex. 88, the interlude originally began with a phrase twice repeated (Ex. 95 a).

95 a. N. II. p. 86.

In a later sketch (Ex. 95 b) it began with a very short contraction.

95 b. N. II. p. 87.

The theme still lacked development to the repetition. This appeared only in the final form (Ex. 95 c), where a series of contractions lead up to the repetition with admirable inevitability.

95 c. Op. 59. III.

As regards the opening theme of the Appassionata (Op. 57), with sixteen bars built on the C-type, I have only to bring together sketch and the final reading, and at once we must be struck by the steadiness of the

79

final form in contrast to the abruptness of the contraction in the sketch.

96. N. II. p. 437.

Op. 57. *Allegro assai.*

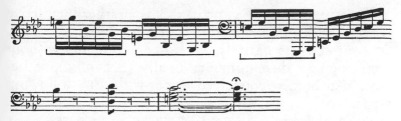

It should be observed also that the C-type finally evolved is again in 16 bars. The development in the presto of the seventh symphony is equally clear.

97 a. N. II. p. 102.

Viola.

97 b. N. II. p. 107.

Presto.

3 times

97 c. Seventh Symphony.

In its first form (Ex. 97 a) this is a rather ineffective S-type with a contractive curtain: later on (Ex 97 b) it consists entirely of two-bar segments without connexion or development: finally (Ex. 97 c), it becomes a boldly conceived type with the following structure:

$$2 + \underbrace{4 \times 2}_{} + \underbrace{2 \times 2 + 2 \times 1}_{} + \underbrace{3 \times 2 + 2}_{} = 24 \text{ bars.}$$

curt. anteced.　　　contin.　　　conclus.

It is clear that Beethoven experienced some difficulty in developing the form; but create it he did by sheer hard work, guided, whether consciously or not, by certain definite principles.

In these last examples we find the development moving towards more wide-embracing thematic complexes. Since Beethoven now preferred to begin themes with sequences, and since such structures tend to involve contraction, a type was produced that begins with a C 8 and then repeats this with a change in the second part. The whole theme, therefore, is of the S-type, in which either the antecedent or the consequent, or both, are of the C-type. I have already referred to an S (C) of this kind from Op. 18. vi (Ex. 87). In Ex. 91 from Op. 1. iii we get the converse type C (S). Both were very common in Beethoven's works, and both tend to increase the complexity of the theme (the thematic complex). I shall mention a few more instances from the S (C) group. As it appears in the sketch, the rondo theme of Sonata Op. 24 has a continuation that is only very slightly developed, whereas in the final form it progresses from half-bar to quarter-bar sequences. The antecedent is a C 8; by means of repetition, with altered and intensified cadence, an S (C) type of 18 bars is produced.

98. N. ii. p. 230.

Op. 24. *Allegro ma non troppo.*

There is a similar development in the theme of the adagio in Sonata Op. 101.

99. N. II. p. 31.

+ Variant.

Op. 101. *Adagio molto.*

&c.

The sketch shows an eight-bar melody, which, to judge from the similarity in the rhythmical structure, was conceived somewhat on the basis of threefold repetition; but it was not to be repeated. The variant introduced a sequence-contraction; but the apex, A flat,

was left in an unfavourable position. The final form
steers clear of this defect and begins the continuation
at once with the contraction and repeats the antecedent
with a different cadence, so that the whole becomes
an S (C) type of 16 bars. The fact that most of the
S (C) types have an even number of bars does not follow
as a matter of course; it is merely a consequence of
what I have often mentioned already, i.e. the regular
number of bars in the types of which it is composed.

Müller-Reuter [1] states (with Czerny as his authority)
that in the conclusion to the first part of the Eroica
there were originally two more bars 'which complete the
rhythmical framework of four bars'. It is quite possible
that the answer to this problem is bound up with Beethoven's attempt to shorten sequences and so to abbre-
viate the rhythmical structure generally. The two bars
referred to are marked by a × in Ex. 100 a.

100 a.   Müller-Reuter, Append. 1, p. 17.

Ex. 100 b gives the whole passage. It is built up as
follows:

$$4+4+4+4+2+2+2+2;$$

interpolation of the two bars would make it:

$$4+4+4+4+2+4+2+2.$$

Accordingly, the present solution seems to be the better
and more justifiable.

100 b.   Third Symphony.

[1] *Lexikon der deutschen Konzertliteratur*, Supplement to Bd. I,
p. 17 et seq.

This suggests an interesting inquiry into the rhythmical construction of Beethoven's compositions in general, i.e. the way in which the larger parts are put together. But obviously such an inquiry would be beyond the scope of the present work.

All the foregoing examples show how the production of form may depend on the cutting out of liaisons, rhythms, sequences, along with the introduction of thematic connexions and sequence-contractions. They make us see the advantage of considering the question from a new angle, and, in place of studying the means by which the remodelling is effected, of demonstrating rather how the first ideas as they appear in the sketches are related to the final form they assume in the finished works, and to what types these belong.

(e) *Transformation of the types.*

I propose to deal first with those themes which develop into an S-type. In Ex. 92 I have already cited the adagio theme of Sonata Op. 96, in which an S is derived from a melody with disconnected liaisons. In

the theme of the trio of the Eroica (Ex. 86) a varied
S-type is developed from a simple one. If we compare
the sketch (Ex. 101 a) with the final form of the adagio
theme in Op. 30. 11, we see a marvellous unfolding from
out a stereotyped form.

101 a.   N, 65. p. 26.

101 b.   Op. 30. 11.
Adagio cantabile.

In the final reading the S-type liaisons almost disappear, or are, at any rate, profoundly modified—at this
stage they cannot be completely destroyed. This theme
shows Beethoven at his most typical; in a later section
I shall discuss more fully the method by which the
transformation is effected. The characteristic feature
in this kind of melodic construction is the remarkable
emotional breadth. It is not common to find hesitancy
such as we get in the scherzo theme of Op. 97. Ex. 102 a
gives the first attempt written as the simplest sort of
S-type, with a very monotonous rhythmical structure.
But the composer has found the right rhythm; and the
way in which he works up this theme to its perfect form
seems, at this stage of the development, to be the
result of logical seriation rather than of imagination.

A second sketch (Ex. 102 b) written in the C-type has sequences in the consequent, but none in the antecedent.

102 b.   N. II. p. 284.

A third (Ex. 102 c) shows the C-type with sequence-contraction, and in this draft the final motive has been found, in addition to the rhythm.

102 c.   N. II. p. 284.

The final form (Ex. 102 d) is a varied S 16.

102 d.   Op. 97.

Scherzo.

We had another instance of this transformation of the C- to the S-type in Ex. 4 from the trio in the eighth

87

symphony (see p. 7). This practically exhausts the list of cases forming the group of changes in form that lead to an S-type. Moreover, it is obvious that a theme with the liaisons characteristic of the C-type cannot straightway be turned into the S-type. For the liaisons in the latter are more fixed and wider in their embrace than in the former; and in the S-type the antecedent and consequent are more closely connected in their first segments.

The reverse change—of the S-type into the C—is therefore more common, especially as the liaisons in the consequent are easily modified by means of sequences. The episodic section in the Sonata Op. 30. ii is a C 8 with sequences in the third, fifth, and seventh bars; the original form was an S 8.

103. Op. 30. ii.

The theme of the minuet in Op. 18. v (Ex. 37) was of a varied S-type in the sketch; but in the final form it is a C 12 with the structure:

$$4 + 2 \times 2 + 4$$

Anteced. Contin. Conseq.

The theme of the presto in the seventh symphony already referred to (Ex. 97) also shows this development. I shall give as my last example the first theme from the sonatina Op. 79. The first sketch (Ex. 104 a) is of the S-type; in a later sketch (Ex. 104 b) the theme is changed, without characteristic liaisons being introduced.

88

104 a. N. ii. p. 269.
Sonate facile.

104 b. N. ii. p. 269.
Presto.

&c.

Finally (Ex. 104 c) an S 8 appears, in which the continuation is added to the antecedent in the form of a sequence.

104 c. Op. 79.
Presto alla tedesca.

Antecedent

Continuation

I shall now refer to some instructive instances in which the sketch belongs to the C-type. When we were considering the up-beat, I mentioned the eight-bar theme of Op. 132 together with the sketches leading up to it (Ex. 19). The final shaping of this theme requires as little further explanation as does the growth of the first theme in the clarinet trio Op. 11 (Ex. 105).

105. N. ii. p. 516.

Op. 11. *Allegro con brio.*

From among the many important instances let me give a sketch for the fifth symphony along with its final form.

106 a.   N. 1. p. 11.
   Sinfonia.   Allo 1mo.

Presto.

&c.

106 b.   Fifth Symphony.
   1st Violin.

2nd Violin.

Violas.

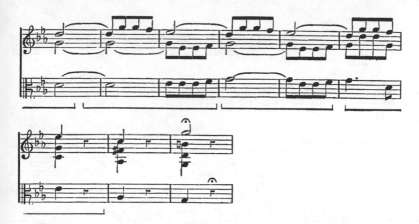

The sketch consists entirely of sequence-like two-bar segments, of which only the last show contraction. The finished form has the structure:

$$5+2\times4+3\times2+2 = 5+16$$
$$\text{curt. anteced. contin. conclus.} \qquad \text{C 16}$$

Schmitz (p. 79) says of this passage, 'We might also imagine it scored as follows:

107. Schmitz, p. 79.

'It is easy to imagine the guiding melodic line as played by the first violins alone, the sustained notes being held by the second violins, violas, and cellos. The imitations . . . as they appear in the actual score, do nothing to alter the rhythmic symmetry of the structure.' But I consider that the regular one-bar rhythm would become too insistent, and would drown the effect of the four-bar sequences. The way in which the form is developed shows that the instrumentation is essential, and determines the structure here; it is not a secondary consideration as Schmitz suggests.

The opening theme of the overture Op. 138 was at first written in seven bars (Ex. 108 a).

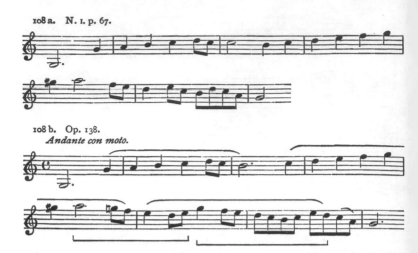

Andante con moto.

Nothing in the consequent corresponds to the sequence in the antecedent. The final form retains the sequence and consists of eight bars. The retention of the first dotted minim throughout all the sketches shows that it was an essential part of the melody; the last note acts both as end and as beginning. Here again, we see the C-type expanded to eight bars. I have repeatedly pointed out that in Beethoven's works the C-type is either 8 or 16 bars in length: and so, as regards the number of bars, it is broadly comparable with the S-type. The latter must of necessity have this number of bars, but the former is not limited in that way. The liaisons characteristic of it are quite different, and Fischer has thoroughly demonstrated the basis on which they rest. Riemann is certainly wrong in thinking that all themes have the S-type as their foundation. This explains, however, why his method of analysis so often does violence to the themes he is considering.

This connexion that exists in Beethoven's music between the two essentially different types explains the important part played in his compositions by the mixed forms, S (C) and C (S), to which I have already referred. Both forms fall in readily with the four-bar structure. They are far wider in their embrace than are the simple

S- and C-types. And it is one of the peculiar features of Beethoven's style that each part of a phrase shall encompass more than do those that precede it.

Let us first consider simple cases where, in an S-type, the antecedent or the consequent is, or both of them are, of the C-type; the result is a mixed type, S (C). We saw an instance of this in the finale theme of Op. 18. vi (Ex. 87), where both antecedent and consequent are C 8. In Ex. 99 likewise we get the development of the adagio theme in Op. 101 to a 16-bar S (C) of the form 8+8. In the theme of the rondo of Sonata Op. 24 (Ex. 98) the subsequent is lengthened so that the S (C) type has 8+10=18 bars. The first theme in Op. 18. 1 is more complicated.

109. Op. 18. 1.

93

The eight-bar antecedent is built up from a triplication (Ex. 62). In the consequent the first four bars are retained and a sequence-contraction of eight bars is added, making it a C 12. It is doubtful whether Schmitz (p. 72) is right in saying that the following nine bars belong to the theme itself; they also contain sequence-contractions. From the repeat we can see that the first eight bars alone constitute a type of melody: it retains only bars 1–8 and then modulates for eleven bars after the manner of bars 21–29. I conclude from this that the theme ends with bar 20. The first draft [1] has the same thematic structure, except that there are nine modulating bars in the repeat; the sketches (Ex. 62) show what difficulty Beethoven experienced in shaping this theme. The bagatelle Op. 26. III furnishes a very beautiful development along these lines. In the sketch (Ex. 110 a) there are no characteristic liaisons whatsoever.

110 a. N. II, p. 199.

110 b. Op. 126. III.

Andante.

Antecedent = C 8

[1] 'Beethovens Streichquartett Op. 18, Nr. 1 und seine erste Fassung.' *Veröffentlichungen des Beethovenhauses Bonn,* II.

94

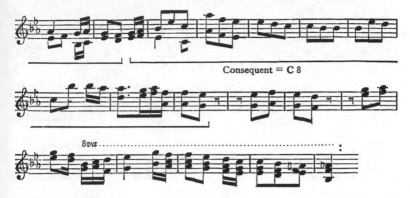

Consequent = C 8

8va ....

From this, by retention of the first four bars and elaboration of the bass motive in bars 10–11, the final form developed a C 8 with a four-bar antecedent and continuation; repetition with modified cadence made this into a sixteen-bar S (C). The postlude is not part of the theme: for the repetition, while varying the theme, fundamentally alters the consequent.

An instance of the converse case (where the whole theme is of the C-type, but its several parts—usually the antecedent—are of the S-type) is shown in the adagio theme of Op. 18. 11. In one sketch, it is true, we see much of what characterizes the final form; but the close juxtaposition of 2 + 3 bars and the very short non-thematic sequence-contractions in bar 5 prevent any feeling of the form coming through. The final draft, with its elaborate structure, is very different.

$$\underbrace{1+2+1+2+}_{\text{anteced.}=\text{S 6}} \underbrace{\|:2:\|+\|:1:\|}_{\text{contin.}} \underbrace{+2}_{\text{conclus.}} = \text{C 14}$$

Here, since the S-type appears cut down to six bars, the C-type has 14 bars instead of 16.

111. N. 11. p. 488.

95

Op. 18. 11.

Adagio cantabile.

Even if we choose to reckon as part of the theme the twelve bars that follow, up to the intervening allegro, this would only mean that the conclusion had also become a C. A theme in Op. 131 shows great complexity of structure, although in the sketch it is merely a simple C 8. In this case also the first four bars are retained and expanded to eight by repetition. These eight bars are repeated with so much alteration in the instrumentation and the accompaniment, and with such different cadences, that we may speak here of an S 16 as antecedent; then follows the 8-bar continuation with contraction.

112 a. N. 11. p. 7.

Allegro.

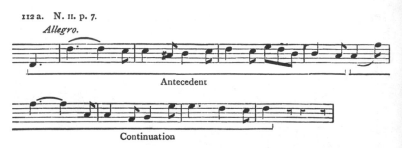

Antecedent

Continuation

Allegro molto vivace.

The sketch shows conclusively that these bars belong
to the theme.

It may be appropriate here to trace the evolution of
the first theme in the adagio of the ninth symphony.
A preliminary sketch is of the C-type (Ex. 113 a), with
an eight-bar antecedent whose articulations are but
little marked.

113 a. N. II. p. 177.

The next sketch substitutes for this a definite S 8
(Ex. 113 b) followed by a continuation.

113 b. N. II. p. 177.

Antecedent = S 8

97

These liaisons are still more schematically shown in a later experiment (Ex. 113 c), where the complete echoes are introduced only after the main sections.

113 c. N. II. pp. 178–9.

Wind instruments

&c.

In the final form (Ex. 113 d) the echoes are shortened but occur more frequently; they are no longer mere interpolations, but aid in the production of form. They constitute a kind of sequence, and so help out to the liaisons: for it is not easy to decide whether the final theme belongs to the S- or to the C-type. As a matter of fact, the two types are completely interwoven in the sketches. Here we are dealing with a theme that is characteristic of Beethoven's mature style; in a later section (Chap. II (g)) I shall attempt to explain the peculiarities that such themes illustrate.

113 d. Ninth Symphony.
Adagio molto et cantabile.

As an example of an unusual development, I may mention the allegro theme of the overture Op. 115. In Ex. 114 a it is composed of seven bars—if an unwritten final note, E flat, be included.

114 a. N. II. p. 15.

It still keeps this number of bars in Ex. 114 b, but now contains sequences, the elements of the C-type.

114 b. N. II. p. 15.

The object of the two following experiments (114 c and d) was to arrive at a different number of bars by means of sequences.

114 c. N. II. p. 16.

114 d. N. II. p. 16.
Presto.

Ex. 114 e gives the result; the theme now runs to nine bars.

114 e. N. II. p. 17.

99

What is unusual, however, is that an S 16 follows this C 9, and is actually in melodic contrast to it. In Beethoven's work this occurs seldom (Gal, p. 68) and it is quite contradictory of Schmitz's principle of 'contrasting derivation'. Finally (Ex. 114 f), the double bars are combined as simple 6/8 time.

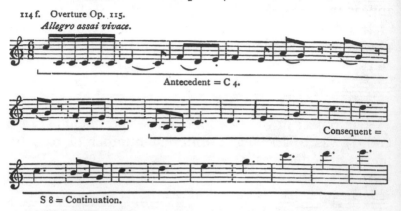

114 f. Overture Op. 115.
Allegro assai vivace.

Antecedent = C 4.

Consequent =

S 8 = Continuation.

The irregularity is retained; the antecedent in the C-type has an apparent length of 5 bars, but as a matter of fact the number of bars is even, for the first is an up-beat or curtain; the high note always lies in the second part of the bar, as is shown by *sf* frequently being written above it in the overture; 114 e is very different in this respect. The dotted bar-lines, therefore, are intended to give the correct number of bars and the stress in the antecedent; in the consequent the reverse occurs. All this may explain why this overture is not accounted one of Beethoven's best works. The process of getting it into shape cost him a great deal of labour, and even in the end he did not achieve a perfect result. The substitution of the S-type for the continuation is not really suitable. Ex. 91 from Op. 1. III gave a case in which the antecedent in a C (S) is an S, and this method of building up the theme gives essentially better results.

What we learn from these and similar examples may be summarized as follows:

1. In addition to the simple S- and C-types, mixed types play an important part in Beethoven's work.

2. The S-type is the only one that is necessarily limited to a length of 8, 16, &c. bars; but the C-type also is usually of this length.

3. This regular number of bars must therefore also appear in the mixed types.

4. Preference for the mixed types tends to enrich and expand the theme.

5. The work of remodelling themes proceeds mainly from the basis given by motives determined from the outset.

6. Accordingly, establishment of the form and of the liaisons that control it must come at a later stage of the work, and only very rarely do these flash on the composer at the first moment in the way the thematic material does.

7. In addition to complete remodelling, the points already mentioned (such as up-beats (p. 13 et seq.) and, in certain circumstances, the position of the melodic apex (p. 27 et seq.)) may be used in the production of form.

(*f*) *Themes with irregular number of bars.*

Before going on to investigate a final characteristic displayed in Beethoven's themes, let me say a word concerning certain themes with an irregular number of bars. It would appear that in many cases special features conceal or counter-balance these irregularities; such examples accordingly serve to strengthen statement 2 above. We can also see the derivation from the sketches. In Ex. 111 we had a theme from Op. 18. II, of the C (S) type and of 14 bars. The antecedent of the song has six bars; the sketch shows the development from four regular ones; the irregularity is scarcely perceptible. The minuet from the trio Op. 1. III (Ex. 91) has as antecedent an S-type of seven bars; it is completed by the addition of a rest to the last bar and of five bars to the continuation that follows. The effect of the whole is to make the irregularity of the several parts less obvious. The original sketch had eight bars, and the same is true of the scherzo theme in Op. 106; whereas in the final form the number of bars is seven. I have already explained why the one bar was taken out (Ex. 24 and p. 67). The first theme of the quartet Op. 18. v (Ex. 54) is also only apparently eleven bars long; the sketch had the structure $4+2+2+2+2$. I have explained that Beethoven

curtain   *a*   *a*

$$\underbrace{}_{\text{S 8}}$$

replaced the note-repetition by a swinging movement, and this involved shortening the curtain by a bar; the actual theme is an S 8. The adagio of the ninth symphony (Ex. 113) is full of repetitions, which involve a new irregularity in the number of bars, an irregularity that does not appear in many of the sketches. I have already drawn attention to the important part these echoes play in form-production; but they have another purpose, and the consideration of this leads me on to yet another feature in Beethoven's style.

(g) *Melodic breadth and elimination of caesurae.*

Wetzel[1] in an account of Kurth's work 'Romantic Harmony' says: 'Bach and Beethoven took great pains to achieve an increasingly perfect rhythmical organization of the succession of sounds in their works. Kurth fails to recognize its development to subtlety from a very obvious foundation. He fails to realize . . . that Bach and Beethoven in their mature years composed melodies without definite limit, which overflowed the strophic limits, and that they were not in the least ashamed of these.' Throughout this chapter we have striven to follow 'these subtle developments to a perfect rhythmical structure' in the case of Beethoven, and, in so doing, to reveal the course he pursued and

---

[1] *Die Musik*, XVI. Jahrgang, p. 267.

the laws that were established; for the liaisons characteristic of the several types of melody are nothing more or less than a rhythmical organization of this kind. Comparison of the sketches and the finished works would also have brought us to the conclusion expressed in Wetzel's second statement.

I have already analysed the remodelling undergone by the theme of the allegro appassionato in Op. 132 (Exs. 6 and 73). The liaisons characteristic of the melodic types form sections separated by caesurae. Normally, the eight-bar S-type has one main caesura between the fourth and fifth bars; and between the second and third or sixth and seventh there are subsidiary caesurae. In the C-type all are distributed in accordance with its structure; sequences naturally tend to involve caesurae of this kind. Now let us consider the effect of such a theme in its final form. The literature on Beethoven is unanimous in its opinion. Helm[1] calls it 'one of the most impressive that he ever discovered'; Thayer (v. 269) writes: 'The melody of the movement is certainly one of the most beautiful that Beethoven ever wrote'. Nothing of all this is apparent in the original sketch (Ex. 6 a); one bar follows the other with a regular rhythm. The sketch Ex. 73 b, on the other hand, has too few liaisons for the production of perfect form. The final reading (Ex. 73 c) has liaisons between bars 1 and 3, but it also carries over from Ex. 73 b bars 4–7, and, in so doing, acquires something essential; except for the caesura between bars 2 and 3, the melody flows on across all the caesurae. And the device that Beethoven employs here is characteristic; repeated notes, which in general he avoids (Chapter I (c)), are introduced in association with unusual rhythms (bars 4–5). In spite of its brevity, the melody seems to flow on interminably. The same thing may be seen in other examples. The bagatelle Op. 126. 1 was at first a varied S-type with marked caesurae in bars 4, 5, and 6.

[1] *Beethovens Streichquartette*, p. 290.

Again in the final form (Ex. 115 b) we find these caesurae bridged by repeated notes and syncopated slurs.

115 b.   Op. 126. I.

At the same time, the subsequent is so markedly altered that it loses its liaisons with the antecedent, and a C 8 is produced. I have already drawn attention to the filling-in of the rest in bar 2 of the slow movement in Sonata Op. 90 (Ex. 1 and p. 5). Now we see that the reason for this was to get rid of the caesura in that bar. Concerning this particular instance Nottebohm remarks (N. II, p. 366) that by the alteration of one note 'the melody is given a significance that it originally lacked'. The change is effected, however, not by this one note alone, but by the repeated note which bridges the caesura. The theme for variations in Sonata Op. 109 (Ex. 26) illustrates the same thing. The sketch still shows clearly the main caesura between bars 4 and 5; in the final form this is bridged by a repeated note and an appoggiatura chord. The way in which this chord is written is not mere chance: it imposes a dynamic connexion with the preceding part of the bar, and —let me once more emphasize this point—it puts the melodic apex in an effective position. Even the delightfully flowing melody of the song 'Mit einem gemalten Band' did not always move so smoothly.

116 a. N. II. p. 286.

Klei - ne Blu - men

gu - te

luf - tig

116 b. Op. 83. III.

Leichtlich und mit Grazie vorgetragen.

Klei - ne Blu - men, klei - ne Blät - ter streu - en

mir mit leich - ter Hand gu - te jun - ge Früh - lings -

- göt - ter tän - delnd auf ein luf - tig Band.

In the sketch (Ex. 116 a) it is clearly of the C-type, with the structure $2 \mid 2+2\times1+2\times\frac{1}{2}+1 = C\,8$. The caesurae in bars 2, 4, 5, and 6 are very conspicuous. In the final form, this is changed. Here the liaisons are weakened, the caesura in bar 4 is got rid of by repetition of a note over the same accompaniment, and that in bar 2 by removal of the rest. The theme of the adagio in Sonata Op. 101, which I have already mentioned (Ex. 99), shows, even in the sketch, an attempt to eliminate caesurae in bars 2 and 4 by means of chromatic progressions that intensify the melody; in bar 6, on the contrary, the caesurae are obvious enough. In the final form these are bridged by sequence-contraction and the unexpected pause, followed by syncopation, on the premature melodic apex. We have here an early example of Beethoven's attempt in this direction, so it is

105

not surprising to find it in a slow movement; for just these movements have always been felt to be especially characteristic of his style.

In the fourth bar of the adagio in Op. 59. 1 the harmonized suspensions (Exs. 52, 78), by means of the tension they produce, bridge to some extent the marked caesurae in the sketch. Here the bridging is made in a forward direction; but in the theme for variations in the violin Sonata Op. 30. 1 the same result is achieved in a backward direction by means of an anticipated entry, as can be seen at a glance when one compares the sketch and the finished work.

117. N. 65. p. 31.

Op. 30. 1.
Allegretto.

The sketch for the theme of the finale in Op. 127 breaks off weakly: it contains only five bars, and is a late example of a theme produced by means of three-fold repetition.

118. N. 11. p. 546.

Op. 127. Finale.

From the fourth bar in the sketch we get bars 4–8 of

106

the final form, and an effect of even, uninterrupted flow. In contrast with the short-winded segments of the beginning, the breadth of the melody is twice as effective; from bar 3 onwards there is no trace left of any caesura.

The foregoing examples and the explanation that I have given of them justify the following conclusions:

1. Melodic breadth is a feature of Beethoven's style as shown in his later works, but it is also to be found in the early slow movements.

2. This breadth is effected, in the main, by elimination of the caesurae characteristic of the particular type of melody.

3. For these he frequently substituted repetition of notes, syncopated liaisons and chromatic melodic progressions.

4. Melodic breadth may call for a certain reduction in the liaisons characteristic of the type, without their being rejected altogether.

5. Beethoven's tendency to introduce lively up-beats (already referred to in Chap. I (*a*)) may have originated in his attempt to give breadth to melody (Ex. 1).

Having reached these conclusions through comparative study, we shall not find it difficult to substantiate them by reference to the finished works. A few examples of this will suffice. In the adagio of Sonata Op. 2. 1 we have an S-type without the caesura in bar 6; the other caesurae in bars 2 and 4 are obvious. The same is true of the largo in Sonata Op. 2. 11.

119. Op. 2. 1.
Adagio.

And to the same category belongs the steady flowing eight-bar theme of the allegretto in Sonata Op. 10. II. The repetitions in the sketch (Ex. 120 b) involve more obvious caesurae; here again we have a development to the eight-bar C-type.

In the first movement of the Moonlight Sonata (Op. 27. II) and in the allegro of Op. 28 the caesurae are obliterated by the regular rhythm used in the accompaniment.

The theme of Sonata Op. 31. III is instructive. Here the melody is full of caesurae, to which the sevenths, with their forward urge, form a marked contrast.

122. Op. 31. III.

As further examples may be mentioned the theme of the first allegro in Op. 74; the minuet from Op. 59. III (Ex. 88), which in spite of being constructed on the S-type shows scarcely any caesurae; the third movement of Op. 18. III; and the slow movement of Op. 18. I, with its accompaniment in triplets. I have purposely chosen early examples: in these Beethoven does not so completely avoid caesurae as he does in the later works already mentioned.

Finally, there is still another method of eliminating the caesurae—i.e. by means of polyphony. Thus in bar 3 of the cavatina from Op. 130 the accompaniment carries on the feeling of movement during the caesura in the violin theme.

123. Op. 130. Cavatina.

In the same way the interpolation marked + at the

beginning of Op. 135 (Ex. 124) bridges polyphonically the halts and rests in the theme.

124. Op. 135.
Allegretto.

(h) The fugue theme.

Considered from this point of view, Beethoven's tendency to use fugato and fugue in his later works takes on a fresh aspect; for nothing is so well adapted to eliminate caesurae and pauses as is fugato, where the new voice can come in just when a caesura would occur. Even in the early works we find experiments of the kind here and there; as, for instance, in the scherzo of Sonata Op. 2. III.

Scherzo. *Allegro.*

Or, again, in the presto of Sonata Op. 10. ii.

126. Op. 10. ii.
Presto.

In considering these movements we see something new, which, however, is on the same lines as the fact of a regular number of bars in the C-type melodies, already referred to. The length of the fugue theme is such that a phrase of 8, 16, or 12 bars results. We can think of the theme from Op. 2. iii (Ex. 125) as evolved from a threefold repetition on the plan $3 \times 2 + 2 = 8$; similarly, the presto theme (Op. 126) has the structure $3 \times 1 + 1 = 4$ in triplicate. The fugue and fugato themes of the later period also show the same regularity in the number of bars. That from Op. 131 (Ex. 10) is in four bars, and is repeated four times in succession.

The fugal working-out in the last movement of Sonata Op. 101 shows an eight-bar theme, the final shape of which depended on sequence-contraction, as is clear from a sketch given by Schenker.[1]

127. Schenker, p. 60.

Op. 101.

The theme of the fugue in Sonata Op. 110 is in four bars, with the structure $3 \times 1 + 1$; an irregularity comes in with the entry of the third part, since the second part lengthens the theme by two bars. The theme of the second movement in the ninth symphony is also in four bars, and it is easy to find other examples in the Missa solemnis and the fugue for string quartet Op. 133.

Of course, we find instances of different structure, such as the irregularity in the entry of the parts in Op. 110, to which I have just referred. But in comparison with the variety in bar-number and number of entries of the fugue themes of Bach's 'Well-tempered Clavichord' we are justified in making some such statement as the following. In Beethoven the theme of the fugue or fugato, and also the passage that involves the entry of the several parts (exposition),

---

[1] *Erläuterungsausgabe der letzten fünf Sonaten, Sonate A dur Op. 101*, p. 60.

usually display the same regular number of bars as do themes of the S- and C-types.

This concludes what I have to say regarding the study of thematic form yielded by a comparison of the sketch with the completed work. Our investigation has shown that in many cases where the motive is retained a great portion of the work is expended on the production of form; our study has yielded us the types and the laws governing these forms, and we have learnt more about them than has been known hitherto. Our study, however, has been based on the works of Beethoven alone; so that for the time being the points we have discovered concerning style must hold good for him alone. We must reserve for a more extensive study the detailed demonstration of the differences between, say, the classical composers of the Viennese school; in the foregoing I have hinted here and there at the lines that this investigation should follow. I believe that, especially as concerns the C-type, it will be found that similar differences occur in the number of bars used for the theme and in the formation of mixed types, as I have already shown they do in the case of the melody based on triplication (p. 46 et seq.). I find support for my view in Essner's[1] observation that 'continuation-types in eight bars are rare among the works of Haydn'.

[1] W. Essner, *Die Thematik des Menuetts in den Streichquartetten J. Haydns*, Diss. Erlangen, 1922.

UNITY WITHIN THE MOVEMENT
AND IN THE COMPLETE WORKS,
WHETHER CONSIDERED SINGLY OR IN GROUPS

(a) Relations within the movement and within the work.

Up to this point we have been concerned with the theme only. But the sketches also give evidence as to the way in which the themes are connected within a movement, in a whole work, or in a group of works. This material enables us to deal with the unity displayed throughout the compositions. Knab [1] has pointed out that the fact that themes are related does not always account for the unity of feeling of cyclical compositions. And in my works on B-A-C-H [2] I have shown that, even after elimination of the similar thematic line, there remain resemblances between the harmonic relations and the figurative elements. But without some sort of preliminary guide we shall find it difficult to discover 'internal' relationships of the kind which are remnants of something originally 'external'. Accordingly those cases are of especial interest in which the sketches show the original relationship of the motives, relationships of which we find but scant traces in the finished works. And we must also be guided by those sketches which permit us to trace the development of several themes from the same material or from the same idea.

[1] A. Knab, 'Die Einheit der Beethovenschen Klaviersonate in As dur Op. 110,' *Zeitschr. f. Musikwiss.*, Jahrg. I.

[2] 'Die Kraft des Themas, dargestellt an B-A-C-H,' *Bach-Jahrbuch*, 1922; and 'B-A-C-H, Stilistisches und Statistisches,' *Zeitschr. f. Musik*, 1925.

As a matter of fact, it is possible to give illustrations of both these methods of treatment. Ex. 128 a shows, in a sketch, a figure from the second theme of Sonata Op. 14. 1, which shows obvious points of resemblance with the first theme.

128 a.   N. II. p. 50.

2nd Theme.

128 b.   N. II. p. 50.

1st Theme.

128 c.   Op. 14. 1.

In both the leap of a fourth is filled in similarly. In the final form (Ex. 128 d) this interpolation in the second theme is changed into a double turn. In the written music especially, this makes the leap much less conspicuous than it was in the sketch, without the internal relation being in any way lost; the double turn may even increase the impetus.

Another alteration in the same movement was made in the motive of the working-out.

129 a.   Op. 14. 1.

&c.

Here it seems to come in as something quite new, though we find from a study of the sketches that it is gradually led up to from an initial motive. In the sketch it is written as in Ex. 129 b; a later experiment altered it to the form in Ex. 129 d.

129 b.   N. II. p. 45.

129 d. N. II. p. 46.

At the same place (as adjunct to the first theme) we find that both sketches contain the final form in quavers (Ex. 129 c).

129 c. Op. 14. I.

In the continuation of motive 129 d there appears 129 e, which obviously derives from it.

129 e. N. II. p. 46.

A later sketch (Ex. 129 f) retains only the first part of this, and makes something new from it, with which we come back very nearly to the pattern of 129 a.

129 f. N. II. p. 49.

Finally, the intermediate segments 129 b, d, e, and f are cut out, and only the ends of 129 a and 129 c remain. Referring to a remark of Brahms [1] I have shown how, by means of latent and sub-conscious work, the motive is made to assume very complicated associations. In Beethoven's sketches we can follow in some cases these undoubtedly unconscious alterations. The first movement of Op. 10. III contains another instance. Ex. 130 a gives the opening of the first theme; judging

[1] P. Mies, *Stilmomente und Ausdrucksstilformen im Brahmsschen Lied,* 1923, p. 7 et seq.

116

from their position, the bars in Ex. 130 b are to be interpreted as leading to a second theme; the origin of the first is obvious, while the figure of the second bar is clearly an abbreviation of the first.

130 a. Op. 10. III.

1st Theme.

130 b. N. II. p. 36.

&c.

The similarity is too great, and in the final form the second theme avoids this (Ex. 12), while retaining the double turn in full. Originally the first theme of the second symphony was written with a dotted rhythm.

131 a. N. II. p. 244.
1st Theme.

131 b. N. II. p. 245.
2nd Theme.

&c.

&c.

In the completed work this rhythm is introduced only in the second theme, their construction on the common chord being sufficient to unite the two themes. In like manner, a dotted rhythm, which in one sketch (N. II, p. 79) was intended for the first theme of the allegro vivace e sempre scherzando in Op. 59. I (♫♪♫ and ♪♫♪), was taken from there and reserved for the contrasting section. Similar changes were made in the minuet of Op. 59. III. Ex. 132 a gives the original form of the first bar, and Ex. 132 b the viola figure of the trio: in the interim, the undulating figure was changed into a scale, and the viola figure was correspondingly modified.

132 a. N. II. p. 86.

132 b. N. II. p. 87.

Viola.

132 c. Op. 59. III.

132 d. Op. 59. III.

fp

There survives only a remote suggestion of their common basis (cf. Exs. 88 and 95). The two rondo themes in the pianoforte concerto Op. 19 show, both as regards their rhythm and their undulating figuration, a similarity which would make them ineffective as themes in one and the same movement (Exs. 133 a and b).

133 a. N. II. p. 69.

&c.

1st Theme.

133 b. N. II. p. 69.

&c.

2nd Theme.

The final form steers clear of both faults. The smooth rhythm of the first disappears (Ex. 133 c); so does, in part, the undulating figure of the second (Ex. 133 d). But later on (Ex. 133 c) the original rhythm of the first theme appears where it usefully serves as a bridge.

133 c. Op. 19.

sf *sf* *sf* *sf* &c.

133 d. Op. 19.

&c.

133 e. Op. 19.

At the end of the Malinconia theme in Op. 18. VI (Ex. 134) there was at first added (Ex. 87 a) a similar ascending figure; an undulating figure followed. From this the final form (Ex. 87 b–d) was then developed.

In all these examples we see the elimination of close relation between the motives of two themes; the result, not at once objectively noticeable, is that the relation is felt as something more internal. I shall refer now to a positively startling instance, in which Beethoven later on reimposed the external relation on the internal. I refer to the transformation of the pianoforte sonata Op. 14. I into a string quartet. From the sound alone, no one could detect any correspondence between the second theme of the last movement of the pianoforte sonata (Ex. 135 c) and the sixth bar of the first theme (Ex. 135 a): but it comes out in the string quartet (Ex. 35 b).

135 b. String Quartet. Op. 41. I.

135 c. Sonata Op. 14. I.

Now we see the similarities—the interval of a third, the succession of the harmonies, the melodic line G, F sharp, G of the piano, to be compared with the second violin part in bar 6. In default of sketches here, it is not possible to say anything positive as to the inner evolution.

Finally, let me add a short series of examples showing the common derivation of different themes in one work. In Ex. 97 a we saw the first sketch for the first movement of the seventh symphony. One of its essential features was the writing of the theme on the common chord. This also appears in a later draft (Ex. 136), which shows a resemblance to the final form, while the first sketch was taken for the third movement.

136. N. II. p. 103.

Before they reached their final form they both had to be pruned of a good many notes belonging to the common chord; naturally, however, this chord still remains recognizable. The melodrama and duet from 'Leonore' show in a quite peculiar way their common issue from the same fundamental form, and also the changes that took place. Let us consider the final form first. Exs. 137 a, b, and c give the beginning of Rocco's part, of Leonore's, and the theme of the accompaniment.

137 a. Prieger, p. 185.
Rocco:
Nur hur - tig fort, nur frisch ge - gra - ben,
es währt nicht lang, er kommt her - ein . . . . .

137 b. Prieger, p. 185.
Leonore:
Ihr sollt ja nicht zu kla - gen ha - ben

137 c. Prieger, p. 184.

The following series (Ex. 137 d), collected from Nottebohm, shows quite clearly how the whole thing is derived solely from the first motive.

137 d. N. II. p. 424.
Nur hur - tig fort

N. II. p. 425.
Nur hur - tig

Nur hur - tig

Nur hur - tig fort

Nur hur - tig

Nur hur - tig

Nur hur-tig   Nur hur-tig

The series is almost without a gap; the interval of
a fourth is the basis of the three final forms, and we see
how the accompanying motive slowly emerges from the
shortening of the first motive into semiquavers.

It is not often that the sketches afford us so deep an
insight into the very foundations upon which rest the
compactness and unity of Beethoven's works. Yet we
may reasonably assume that in many other instances for
which the evidence of the sketches is lacking the works
were constructed on a similar basis, which we can do
no more than sense. There are far too many links
between the final drafts that we have before us.
However conscientious our intellectual analysis, it is
not able to follow the ceaseless activity of the creative

imagination. I consider, therefore, that all the more importance attaches to the examples I have given; they reveal an essential principle guiding his creative work.

(*b*) *Relations within a group of works.*

We must therefore not be surprised to find the same germ developing in several different compositions. Nottebohm has already drawn attention to derivations of this kind. I do not consider that we are dealing here with actual self-plagiarisms, but that the same mental state induced the construction of themes with melodic and rhythmical resemblances. It is possible to point to several developments of the kind which follow totally different directions. Here it is interesting to compare the passages brought together in Ex. 138; in both, the melodic line of the antecedent is the same.

138 a. N. 65. p. 9.

138 b. Op. 18. IV.
Menuetto. *Allegretto.*

138 c. Op. 22.
Menuetto.

Riemann has also remarked on their affinity, at any rate as far as concerns the first two passages (Thayer, ii. 190). It is worth while considering the different types of melody to which the same antecedent leads. In the sketch this is a poorly defined S-type, in Op. 18. IV it is a varied S-type, in Op. 22 it is the C-type; but all three are in eight bars. The theme of the G major variations shows correspondence, as regards its first motive, with the rondo of Sonata Op. 22.

139 a. Variation. G major.
Andante quasi Allegretto.

139 b. Op. 22.

Here also the different development is worthy of note; the theme for the variations is given as an S-type, and the sequences in the episodic passage are immediately shortened. Ex. 140 a reproduces the theme of the second movement of the violin sonata Op. 24, as it appears in a sketch-book which, in addition to drafts for this sonata, also contains a passage from the quartet Op. 18. 1. It would seem that at this time the quartet was changed from the original form [1] and remodelled. The rhythmical structure in Ex. 140 a is the same as at the beginning of the quartet (Ex. 140 b). The re-shaping of the slow movement of Op. 24 then shows beautifully the development towards 'cantabile'—the elements underlying which, according to Fischer (pp.

[1] *Veröffentlichungen des Beethovenhauses II. Beethovens Streichquartett Op. 18. 1 und seine erste Fassung.*

48, 50), are (1) repose in the more accented part of the bar, (2) lively up-beats, and (3) sustained ends to the motives; the final form brings this out very clearly.

140 a. N. ii. p. 234.
Adagio.

140 b. Op. 18. 1.
Allegro con brio.

140 c. Op. 24.
Adagio molto espressivo.

Two associated sketch-books of the year 1798–9 contain the themes for the rondo Op. 51. ii and for the quartet Op. 18. ii.

141. N. ii. p. 478.

Rondo. Op. 51. ii.
Andante cantabile e grazioso.

Juxtaposition of the two sketches and the final forms (Exs. 141 and 55) brings out clearly the similarity in the spirit of tenderness and 'gallantry' with which both themes are imbued; in discussing Ex. 55, I pointed out how this character becomes intensified as we proceed from the sketch; and the theme of the rondo shows precisely the same development. The opening theme of the G major concerto Op. 58 displays similarities with the first theme of the fifth symphony, and originally the figure of the accompaniment in the rondo of the same concerto was still more closely related to that in the prisoners' chorus in the 'Leonore'. This likeness was so marked that Nottebohm was led to ask: 'Would Beethoven have written the first movement of the G major concerto if he had not written the C minor symphony?' (N. 1, p. 13), and again: 'Would Beethoven have written the prisoners' chorus as he did if he had not also written the G major concerto?' (N. 1, p. 14).

The parallel example given above from Op. 18. 1 and Op. 24 (Ex. 140) showed a divergent development from a similar rhythmical construction, into a slow movement on the one hand and into an allegro on the other. If now we look at the completed theme in the adagio of the E flat major concerto Op. 73 (Ex. 142 a) and that of the military march in F major (Ex. 142 c), it is really impossible to detect that they are derived from two sketches that were rhythmically identical (Exs. 142 b and 142 d). The sketches come from the same book.

142 a. Op. 73.
Adagio un poco mosso.

142 b. N. II. p. 256.

142 c. March. F major.

142 d. N. II. p. 258.
Marcia.

Themes showing similarities in melodic and rhythmical treatment may be traced to the same period of composition, which, within certain limits, we may imagine to have been a period dominated by a certain mental state. And this will likewise account for the similarity in character displayed by certain entire works. Scattered through the sketch-book for the Eroica (N. 80) we find, among other things, drafts for the three marches written for four hands, Op. 45, and also for some unknown marches. If we link up with this the fact that the third symphony itself contains the funeral march and the march-like episode in the last movement, it is easy to suppose that in these various works with a march character we are dealing with different precipitations, as it were, of the same idea. An idea of the kind may be quite external and yet have great internal importance.

Nottebohm (N. 80, p. 58) mentions finger exercises for the pianoforte, and considers that preoccupation with a technical matter such as this would have influence on a work composed soon afterwards—the Sonata Op. 53, for instance. If we compare with this the often very 'showy' technique of the andante in F major, which originally belonged to the C minor sonata, we seem to find here an irradiation from the same idea. If we are to believe Ries, the removal of the F major andante took place as follows (Leitzmann, p. 73): 'A friend of Beethoven expressed his opinion that the sonata was too long, and was violently criticized by him for saying so. It was only afterwards, when my master thought the matter over calmly, that he saw the justice of the remark. He then published the big andante in F major (3/8 time) by itself, and also composed the interesting introduction to the rondo, as we have it to-day.' And we have something of the same kind, though in a matter connected with the technique of form, when Beethoven, in the course of composing the fugue in the cello sonata Op. 102. II, wrote a whole series of fugue themes in his sketch-book. Nottebohm has brought together six of these (N. II, p. 319). Here again we see the attempt, doubtless quite instinctive, to shape and test the same idea in a number of different directions.

What I have been saying explains some things which otherwise are scarcely intelligible, and which in a lesser composer would be fatal. Nottebohm (N. II, p. 27) shows that in the last movement of the trio in Op. 1. II Beethoven has combined melodies which originally did not belong to one another. He explains how the slow movement of Sonata Op. 30. III arose by bringing together a number of melodies from different sources. A series of sketches (N. II, p. 404 et seq.) reveals the remarkable fact that the slow introduction to the overture Op. 124 originally had an allegro quite different in construction. The alla danza tedesca belonged at first to the A minor quartet (Thayer,

v. 293); in Ex. 59 I gave a sketch for it in A major. There is a close correspondence between the beginning of the A minor quartet Op. 132 and the fugue for string quartet Op. 133, which was the last movement of the B flat major quartet Op. 130; again the sketches show that they were written at the same time (N. 11, p. 550). All this would seem 'composition with a vengeance', as Nottebohm says in discussing Op. 30. 111, if it were not that what we have learnt from the foregoing instances gives us an explanatory clue. The similarity in the state of mind that produced the several melodies and movements gave them so much in common and so close an internal relationship, that it was very easy to effect their association and interchange. The common objective basis is not so easy to demonstrate here as in the previous examples given in this section; but nevertheless it is there. And probably we should also take account of the important fact, on which I have already so often insisted, i.e. that Beethoven always worked on several movements and whole compositions simultaneously. Karl von Bursy reports him as saying (Leitzmann, p. 162): 'No, I do not work on uninterruptedly like that at any one thing. I always work on several together; now I take up one, and now another.' Schlösser vouches for the same thing (Thayer, iv. p. 420), and the sketches reveal it clearly. But undoubtedly the result was a certain common emotional basis for the works thus simultaneously developed, which admitted the transferences I have mentioned to be made without imperilling the unity of the whole. And I should be inclined to see in this method of enforcing unification a specific characteristic of Beethoven as a composer. But it explains why we find it so difficult to demonstrate the objective basis, though we can feel at once that it is there.

But that even Beethoven could not always undertake such remodelling without disturbing the unity of a composition is shown by the violin sonata Op. 47, of which the tarantella-like last movement originally belonged to Sonata Op. 30. 1. A certain 'showiness' is common to the three movements in the former sonata. The note in the title, 'Sonata scritta in uno stilo molto conzertante, quasi come d'un conzerto', and the fact that it was written for the virtuoso Bridgetower (Thayer, ii. 410), are the outward signs of this. But in my opinion the three movements do not attain to real inward unity. 'As a matter of fact, Beethoven was for once compelled to depart from his custom of allowing the idea to come slowly to maturity' (Thayer, ii. 298 et seq.); consequently the association was effected in rather a superficial way. And still less happy perhaps was the interpolation of the final movement in the B flat major quartet Op. 130—a movement composed afterwards and substituted for the final fugue. Under pressure from the publishers (Thayer, v. 298 et seq.) he set to work again on the last movement at Gneixendorf in 1826. A long interval had elapsed since the composition of Op. 130; perhaps also he intentionally wished to avoid the serious character of the final fugue. The movement he composed is genuine Beethoven; yet Thayer says (v. 407): 'It failed to incorporate the ideal that he saw in the B flat major quartet; what he was striving after was youth and inward happiness. We share his feeling, but we must confess that the movement does not quite fit into the frame of the B flat major quartet.'

The analyses in this section, however, have shown how the unity in Beethoven's works arises from his method of composition. The objective foundations of this unity have been revealed in a number of examples in which we see different developments from similar beginnings, and finally, we have been able to find an explanation for some unusual cases in the technique of composition. It is the sketches which have made these conclusions possible.

IV
CONSTANT FEATURES IN THE DEVELOPMENT

CONCERNING Beethoven, Bettina Brentano wrote (Leitzmann, p. 116): 'He does not work like Winter, the conductor, i.e. write the thing down just as it first occurs to him. He lays out a plan on broad lines and arranges his music in a certain form, and in accordance with that he proceeds to work.' And Braun von Braunthal (Leitzmann, p. 335) tells us of a conversation with Schubert in an inn where Beethoven also was sitting. 'From time to time he took a second and larger notebook from the inner pocket of his coat and wrote in it with his eyes half shut. "What is he writing?", I asked. . . . "He is composing", was his answer. "But he is writing words, not notes." "That is the way he works. He uses words to describe the course of the ideas for this or that composition, and at most intersperses them with a few notes."' And, among other things, Schlösser reports Beethoven as saying: ' . . . and since I am conscious of what I am aiming at, I never lose sight of the idea. It grows and rises up before me; I hear and see the image of it standing there before my mind as of one cast.' And in the sketches we can see ideas of this kind developing in the most various ways. But in studying them we must follow the reverse direction. Hitherto chief place has been given to the alterations; in what follows, we must keep our attention on what remains unchanged, even in those cases where there has been a great deal of remodelling.

(a) Constancy in the treatment of motive and rhythm.

I shall deal first with what persists of the treatment of motive and rhythm, however extensive the alteration. Nottebohm has already pointed out that two sketches of a melody for the middle section of the presto in

Op. 74 show a similarity with the score 'as regards the type of notes chosen'.

143 a.   N. 11. p. 94.

143 b.   N. 11. p. 94.

&c.

143 c.   Op. 74.

Più presto quasi prestissimo.

Si ha s'immaginar la battuta di §.

There is also unquestionable resemblance in the way the line flows, though in the final reading the sequences are better shaped. A purely rhythmical idea led to the bagatelle Op. 126. vi. In the sketch (N. ii, p. 204) there appear the beginnings of pieces in three-bar rhythm, along with the remark, 'auch Rhitmus von 3 Takt'. Except for this three-bar structure there is nothing in the final form to relate it to the sketch, either with regard to motive or anything else. Ex. 144 b gives the alternative for the bagatelle Op. 126. iv as it appears in the sketch; in the final form nothing is retained but the syncopations and the pedal-points.

144 a. N. ii. p. 202.

144 b. Bagatelle. Op. 126. iv.

In these examples we are dealing, it is true, with single instances: but it is possible to determine two main groups. In the first of these groups the boundaries of the melody and the course the line follows are the same. The first sketch for the funeral march in the Eroica, if we except the surviving initial bars, shows the occurrence of the apex A flat towards the end. Compare Ex. 145 with Ex. 56.

145. N. 80. p. 37.

&c.

The beautiful episode in the first movement of the Eroica (Ex. 146 a) is derived from a threefold repetition of the motive with the initial notes G—G flat—G (Ex. 146 b) or G—G—G flat (Ex. 146 c).

146 a. Third Symph.

Ob.   Cl.   Fl.   Viol.   Ob.

Cl.   Fl.   Viol.   Ob.

Cl.   Tutti.

146 b. N. 80, p. 7.

146 c. N. 80, p. 9.

&c.

The last of these sketches fills in the large repetitions with smaller ones, and from this is developed the next sketch (Ex. 146 d)—a much more varied form, in which, however, the constructional plan 3 × 4 is very schematic.

146 d. N. 80, p. 11.

134

It is only in later sketches that the last section is given its forceful ending in unison, with contraction of the rhythm. This is an interesting example of how, within a given rhythmical structure and a given line for the main notes, a melody becomes strengthened as regards form and emotional content. In a sketch and in the final form of the aria 'O wär ich schon mit dir vereint', the extreme points and the cadence correspond; but in other respects the two drafts are quite unlike.

147. N. 80. p. 67.

O wär | dich. nen - nen !

Prieger, p. 21,

Still more numerous are the instances in which the melodic movement in notes of the common chord persists as the foundation both of the sketch and of the final form. In my study of Brahms' songs [1] I have shown how the building of the melody on the common chord serves there a perfectly definite purpose in expression. Now, when we find Beethoven retaining this thematic structure, even with very considerable change in the motives, it must mean that this had some special meaning for him. In a later section [Chap. VII (a)] I shall attempt to elucidate this point; here I shall merely give the most important examples. There are numerous sketches for the march with chorus 'Schmücket die Altäre' from the 'Ruins of Athens'. From these (Ex. 148 a) the instrumental melody of the march was developed (Ex. 148 b); they are all based on the common chord.

[1] Op. cit., p. 110 et seq.

Schmückt die Al - tä - re   Sie sind ge - schmückt

Schmückt die Al - tä - re   Sie sind ge - schmück - et

Schmück - et   die   Al - tä - re

N. II. p. 142.

Schmückt   die   Al - tä - re

148 b.   The Ruins of Athens, Op. 113.

Sketches for the song 'Der freie Mann' show the same thing (Ex. 149).

149.   N. II. p. 561.

Wer,   wer   ist . . .   ein   frei - er   Mann

N. II. p. 562.

Final form.

Wer,   wer   ist ein   frei - er   Mann?

And sketches for the 'Dona nobis pacem' from the Missa solemnis turn throughout on the ascending or descending common chord (Ex. 150).

150.   N. II. p. 464.

do - na   no - bis

do - na

pa . . . . cem pa . . . .

do - na no - bis

Belonging to this category of instrumental melodies I may mention the pianoforte concerto in E flat major (Op. 73). In beginnings for this as they occur in the sketches (Ex. 151 a), the descending common chord is again and again conspicuous, and this is carried over into the final form (Ex. 151 b).

151 a.   N. II. p. 501.

&c.

151 b.   Op. 73.

The determining factor here may be the heroic character of the theme (do not let us forget the connexion of this concerto with the march in F major). The examples from the 'Ruins of Athens' and the song 'Der freie Mann' are also written on lines expressing pomp and power.

(b) *Modulation*.

Modulation, consisting either in a general modulation plan or in the introduction of new keys singly, is one of the constant features in the course of development from sketch to final form. Thus, in the F major movement, vivace alla marcia, in the Sonata Op. 101, the introduction of the key A major was predetermined. If we are to judge by the remark, 'Erster Teil in A ohne : ||: repet' (N. 11, p. 340), the first part was to end in that key; the plan was changed to the extent that the second part began in A major. In the same way, it was planned beforehand that, in the middle part of the first theme of the andante in F major, the key of D flat major should be introduced (N. 80, p. 61). The conclusion of this piece was to contain G flat major (Ex. 152 a); it was only later on that the main theme appeared in that key (Ex. 152 b).

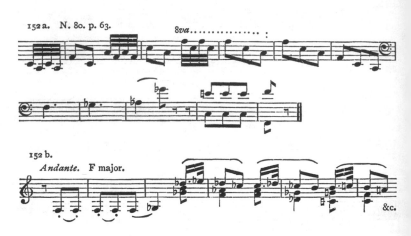

152 a. N. 80. p. 63.

152 b.
Andante. F major.

We find the same Neapolitan key touched upon in a sketch for the end of the scherzo of Op. 106 (N. 11, p. 131); in the final form the deviation is slightly extended. Up to this point we have considered only short excerpts; but we shall find that for the larger parts plans for modulation were also laid down and adhered to. Thus Beethoven sketched the prelude to the last movement of Op. 106 in the form Ex. 153, which gives the plan in full; the episodic portions, on the other hand, were inserted at the points I have marked with an asterisk.

In the first large sketch for the first movement of the Eroica (N. 80, p. 7) the course of the modulation is determined in its broad outline, although much work was still required for the shaping of the several parts. Again and again Beethoven attacked the prelude to the last movement. Concerning this, Nottebohm says (N.80, p. 51): 'All the drafts are different, but they agree in opening with the dominant of G minor and in reaching the dominant of E flat major'. Here also we may reckon those instances in which the march of the bass is retained. In the sketches for the Sonata Op. 2.1 (Ex. 154 a) it is not difficult to recognize the final form.[1]

[1] We must imagine the addition of a flat to the key-signature in the sketch.

And in the slow movement of the Sonata Op. 30. III
nothing is retained of the projected melody but the
march of the bass, as can be seen at once on comparing
the sketch (Ex. 155 a) and the final form (Ex. 155 b).

155 a. N. 65. p. 31.

&c.

155 b. Op. 30. III.

It is obvious that this swaying, rhythmically contrasted
plan, must determine the character of the melody. Here
again we see by what unusual detours the unification
of Beethoven's works was often effected. The most
extensive of these persistent plans for modulation is to
be found in the first finale of the 'Leonore'. Concerning
this Nottebohm says: 'Both in the sketch and in the
printed form the first words of the second melody "Wir
müssen gleich zum Werke schreiten" are in E flat
major, the last words "Wir folgen unsrer strengen
Pflicht" are also in E flat major, the first words of the
following entry "O Vater, eilt" are in C minor, and
the last words "Ja wir gehorchen schon" are in the
dominant of D minor. But the themes or melodies given
to these words are quite different in the sketch from what
they are in the printed form.' Here I merely lay stress
on the fact and its importance for the development of
the whole; later on [Chap. VII (d)] I shall proceed to
discuss whether we have to do with an idea based on

some fundamental character of the keys themselves. The examples we have dealt with make it probable that the course of modulation in Beethoven's work was to some extent determined from the outset. The sketches published by Nottebohm enable us to follow this in detail only in a relatively small number of cases.

(c) *Instrumentation.*

Now and then the idea of some definite instrumentation determines the line of development. Nottebohm (N. 80, p. 48) speaks of the various drafts for the scherzo trio of the Eroica; the fourth alone paves the way for the final form; but in all the sketches a prominent part was destined for the three horns. And of the original sketch for the last movement of the Sonata Op. 53 only the beginning, which is based on the pedal effect, was carried over into the final form, as is shown by comparison of the sketch and the completed work (Ex. 156).

156 a. N. 80. p. 63. Rondo.

&c.

156 b. Op. 53. Rondo.
Allegretto moderato.

(d) *General plans.*

But in the original drafts there are ideas of still wider compass, which we find again in the final form. In

141

several of the works containing variations the first bars of these are noted down with their characteristic figuration, and in this way a brief plan of the whole is put together. This is true, for instance, of the variations on the theme 'Une fièvre brûlante' (N. II, p. 30), and also of the variations in D major Op. 76 (N. II, p. 273), the variations in the Sonata Op. 57 (N. II, p. 441) and, in part, of those in the Sonata Op. 111.[1] As an example I shall give a sketch of this kind for the variations in G major, always placing before the final form the sketch and the observations accompanying it.

---

[1] H. Schenker, *Erläuterungsausgabe der letzten fünf Sonaten, Op. III*, pp. 58–9, 64.

It would appear, then, that Beethoven carried out the plan in some exactitude; it is interesting to observe his avoidance of note-repetition in the first variation. We may also consider here the plan for the last movement of the Eroica, which Nottebohm gives, with the remark: 'According to this, it was intended that the whole movement should have an introduction beginning on the dominant of G minor; the theme in the bass was at first to be unisono, and then worked up by variation and fugue; then a slow movement was to follow, having the melody of the theme in the upper part, &c. Roughly speaking, this is the course followed in the printed score.' Nottebohm also gives a similar plan for the three last movements of Sonata Op. 106, 'which, as regards the words, if not the notes, was followed almost exactly in the final reading' (Ex. 158).

158. N. II. p. 129.

First Minuet.   End.

Adagio.   F sharp minor or F sharp major. Treated as a fugue.

B flat minor wherever possible.

Three further examples lead us into the realm of poetry and beyond the purely musical concept. I may as well mention them now, as they will be of some importance later on. From the sketches and notes brought together here—selected, of course, by Nottebohm—we can see how the word 'pacem' creates a realistic conception.

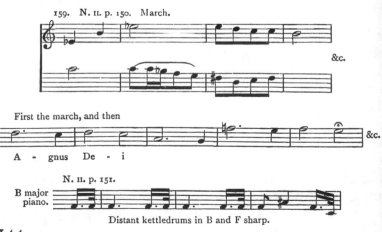

159. N. II. p. 150.   March.

&c.

First the march, and then

A - gnus De - i

&c.

N. II. p. 151.

B major piano.

Distant kettledrums in B and F sharp.

 the Agnus Dei begins just here.  *recit.* miserere, miserere Agnus Dei

Above everything, a tremendous sense of inward peace ... Victory!

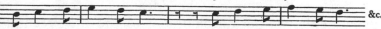 &c.

dona nobis pacem representing peace, both *within* and *without*.

This idea is the foundation for the march, for the use of tympani, for the recitative, and finally for the observation 'representing peace, both within and without'. In the final form of the Missa solemnis this changed to 'Prayer for peace, both within and without'. The same thing occurred in the case of the introduction to the ode 'An die Freude' in the ninth symphony. It has often been shown—for instance, by Schindler [1], who also published sketches, and by Graf [2] (p. 80 et seq.)—what were the experiments made by Beethoven in his attempt to get an effective entry for the chorus. I shall deal with this point very briefly here. At first it was obviously intended 'to begin the finale with an independent thematic instrumental introduction, and then to let the chorus come in, either forthwith, or after the melody expressing joy, which was to be played by the orchestra, at first very simply and then in greater variety' (N. II, p. 186). Then the words 'Let us sing Schiller's immortal song' were inserted. Meanwhile came the idea to introduce the beginnings of the several movements between the recitatives, so that the text ran somewhat as follows (N. II, p. 190): 'This is a day of jubilee, worthy to be sung ... (theme of the first movement). O no, that won't do; I want something more pleasing (theme of the second movement). That is no better, merely rather more cheerful (theme of the third movement). This is also too tender. Must find something more rousing, like the ... I'll sing you something myself ... (theme of

[1] A. Schindler, *Biographie von L. v. Beethoven*, 1840, p. 139 et seq.
[2] See list of abbreviations.

145

the fourth movement). That will do! Now I have found something to express joy.' In this we find points agreeing with the unison passages of the final form. The dots represent illegible passages. By abbreviating the text and retaining the idea by means of the instruments, we get development to the final reading. 'Oh my friends, these sounds won't do! Let us have something more pleasant and more joyful.' And Beethoven intended to give rein to one of these fundamental ideas in the plan for an opera, concerning which he writes (N. ii, p. 329): 'Perhaps the dissonances throughout the whole opera might not be quite resolved, or else in some totally different manner, for our civilized music cannot be conceived in such weird and desolate times.'

BEETHOVEN AS CREATIVE ARTIST

It may be true that the last examples, considered separately, are not so suitable to guide us in our analysis of Beethoven's style as was the line of study pursued in the first three chapters; nevertheless, they offer us a quite exceptional opportunity for becoming acquainted with his manner of working. In what follows I shall attempt to give some idea of these methods and of the importance that the sketches had for him; and I shall base my remarks on detailed study of the sketches and on the information gleaned from Beethoven himself and from the reports concerning him given by others. Spitta[1] and Riemann[1] and A. Heuss[1] have done something of the same kind, and we have also some disconnected observations by Nottebohm. But the contradictions revealed in the works of these authors make the problem one that is still worth considering.

(*a*) *Writing the sketches.*

The writing of sketches went on all the time. H. Anschütz (Leitzmann, p. 237) tells us of a meeting with Beethoven. 'I saw lying in the meadow a man, rather untidily dressed, who supported his head on his left hand—a head weighed down by thought, very spiritual, and beautiful in a wild sort of way. His eyes were fixed on a sheet of music, and on this he drew with his right hand heavy, mystical characters, drumming with his fingers in the intervals.' I have already mentioned another scene in a tavern; and von Breuning gives us Beethoven's own words (Leitzmann, p. 333):

[1] See list of abbreviations.

'I always carry about a note-book like this, and if an idea comes to me I make a note of it at once. I even get up in the night when something occurs to me, for otherwise I might forget the idea.' Schindler [1] tells us the same thing—'One day when we were walking with Beethoven and his nephew in the beautiful Helenental near Baden, Beethoven told us to walk ahead a little way. Soon after, he called us back again, remarking that he had now noted down two motives for an overture.' From the size of many of the sketch-books, however, and from the fact that ink has been used throughout them, we may feel certain that these served for work at home (N. 65, p. 11). Nottebohm has also pointed out that the sketches, taken in series, do not always reflect the order of composition. 'It was Beethoven's custom, when he attacked a new piece, to take a new page for it and to leave the preceding pages empty for the alteration or completion of some work previously begun. If he were working at the two compositions simultaneously or alternatively, and could find no more room to carry on the second one, it sometimes happened that the parts he had left free for it got used up: and so finally the sketches for different compositions became intermingled.' It seems to me, for instance, that the sketches for the trio Op. 97 published by Wetzler [2] do not correspond with the order suggested: the facsimile suggests rather that, after proceeding with several fragments, he finally wrote the melody on the upper right-hand portion of the page (No. 2 in Wetzler's series). I have referred to Beethoven's peculiar habit of working on several pieces and movements simultaneously, and I have drawn attention to the importance of this fact for the unity of his works, whether considered singly or in groups.

Another peculiar feature is the length of time taken

[1] Quoted from F. Kerst, *Die Erinnerungen an Beethoven*, 1913, Bd. I, p. 269.
[2] *Die Musik*, Jahrgang XVI, p. 163.

to bring many of the compositions to full maturity. He worked on the ninth symphony for six years, and on the Missa solemnis for four. He attacked other works at very different times. There are sketches for the setting of Matthison's 'Opferlied' with dates between 1794 and 1822, and those for the song 'Ich war bei Chloë' range from 1798 to 1822. We can trace the idea for the 'Ode an die Freude' from 1793 to 1822, and attempts at the overture Op. 115 can be found in the sketch-books of the years 1809, 1811, 1812, and 1814. The theme of the Sonata Op. 111 occurs in a sketch-book as early as 1801–2 (N. 65, p. 19); the theme for the pastoral symphony, which dates from 1807–8, is to be found in sketches of the year 1803 (N. 80, p. 55).

There can be no doubt also that Beethoven looked through the sketch-books from time to time. Heuss has explained this fact (p. 242) by saying that Beethoven 'after making great mental effort to bring before his spiritual vision, in the form of a symphony or an overture, some subject—whether he called it Bonaparte, or Leonore, or Coriolanus, or some such name—now required music and, more particularly, fundamental musical concepts, in order to give artistic expression to this idea. . . . He went for his sketch-books and looked through them. Suddenly his eye, alight with his idea, lit on one of these first inspirations, and discovered in the primitive language of music what he had seen with his mental vision.' Here Heuss has divided into two parts the foundation of Beethoven's shaping process—the primitive musical motive and the idea. Detailed study of the sketches must naturally concern itself with this double foundation; and Riemann, in particular, would have been spared many mistakes if he had not been too much wrapped up in his theory of musical ideas.

(b) Artistic creation.

I consider, however, that Heuss's understanding of the

nature of the idea is too narrow. In my opinion, nothing can better help us to a complete picture of Beethoven's method of work than a brief statement of the analysis of artistic creation and aesthetic judgement on the lines followed by Meumann.[1] In his 'System der Aesthetik' he distinguishes three main motives in artistic creation. (1) Some experience that affects the artist in a greater or less degree and stimulates his mental life, (2) the urge compelling the artist to express what he has experienced (the expression-motive), and (3) the making of it something permanent by putting it in a concrete form appreciable by the senses through the medium of some definite art (representation- or work-motive, form-motive) (p. 47). But the expression-motive dominates human life in other departments as well: so Meumann comes to the conclusion 'that the representation-motive, and not the expression-motive, is what really counts with the artist' (p. 56). And he goes on to state (pp. 58–9): 'And one of the most interesting facts concerning artistic creation is that these two motives are in a certain degree hostile (antagonistic) to one another.' 'The effort to represent what he has experienced in a permanent form, and in a particular artistic form, must here as elsewhere inevitably tend to dam back and restrict the effort towards emotional expression; conversely, the effort to express emotion is continually striving to hamper the development of an actual work of art in strict artistic form.' I can scarcely believe that, in setting up this theory, Meumann ever thought of Beethoven and his sketches. But when we consider them in this light they seem to give double force to his penetration. The motive the composer receives from his imagination as his reaction to some experience, and hastily entrusted by him to his sketchbooks—this is the expression-motive. To shape this into a work of art required a struggle, the scene of which, as we clearly see, was only too often the sketch-

[1] See list of abbreviations.

book—a struggle with the idea. This idea, however, must not be too closely restricted, in the way Heuss would restrict it; it is the work-motive, the form-motive itself. It may be a positive idea: the 'Dona nobis pacem' of the Missa solemnis, the ode 'An die Freude', the 'weird' dissonances of the projected opera (p. 146), are all of this kind: so are Bonaparte and the rest. But the other constant developmental features discussed in Chapter IV are also to be regarded as work-motives. And finally, we may include here the style determinants culled from the alteration groups and dealt with in the first three chapters. They all help to give an artistic form to the expression of the original motive, and just the form that corresponded to the spirit of Beethoven. What Schlösser tells us concerning Beethoven's thought seems to me especially clear when considered from this point of view (Thayer, iv. p. 420). 'I alter a great deal, discard it and try again until I am satisfied. And then inside my head I begin to work it out, broadening it here, restricting it there, deepening it and heightening it; and since I am conscious of what I am trying to do, I never lose sight of the fundamental idea. It rises up higher and higher, and grows before my eyes until I hear and see the image of it, moulded and complete, standing there before my mental vision.' The idea was conscious; but this does not mean that Beethoven could have expressed it in words. His own particular representative- and form-motives, which were of a poetical kind, hovered before him; they rose and grew higher and higher; and when a complete union was achieved between them and the expression-motive there remained 'only the work of setting them down, which went very quickly'. The sketch-books show that this working out went on not only in his head, but also on paper. And the ascent and growth of the idea did not proceed in a straight line, or, so to speak, logically, as would actually happen if it were simple, definite, and established; it had to follow many crisscross routes. The sketches for the variations in Op. 127 (N. ii, p. 210 et seq.) contain a very obvious example of this: I shall give the circumstances, and in Spitta's words (p. 188). 'The adagio, with the variations that follow it, belongs to the most beautiful of the inspired songs such as only Beethoven could write, songs in which the soul, freeing itself from all earthly tribulation, rises up towards what is eternal. It would seem impossible that any sound from earth could penetrate this calm and serene air. But we find that Beethoven, after he has worked on the adagio for a time, is suddenly possessed by his daemon. He changes the key and the tempo, and the theme becomes a gay allegro movement, through which his humour goes leaping merrily. And, as is indicated by the long continuance of the movement, he seems to have seriously intended to bring this in as an independent part of the quartet.' Riemann also points out (Thayer, v. p. 149) the connexion between the piece with the superscription 'la gaieté' and the variations. Spitta aptly compares this phenomenon with the sudden emotional changes so characteristic of Beethoven's own life. We get a similar example in final form, shown by the sharp contrast between the allegretto and the Malinconia theme in the last movement of Op. 18. vi (Exs. 87 d and 134).

The basic idea had to find its suitable expression-motive, and the motive had to have the necessary adaptability in order to correspond to the idea. It is possible to explain Beethoven's rejecting so many themes only on the supposition that in such cases he found it impossible to get the required unity of expression and form. For, in themselves, these themes do not seem inferior to many that he used. The more 'special' the idea—I might even say, the less it belonged to the domain of music—the more difficult it must have been to effect this unity. The sketches give us instances in which themes were fundamentally altered but still retained their original character; this can be seen clearly when we compare with the final form the sketch for the theme of the finale in Op. 18. III; the final form still retains the hurried jerkiness (Ex. 22). In the same way, the projected final theme of Sonata Op. 57 keeps the restless semiquaver movement shown in the original sketch.

160. N. II. p. 441.

8va............................:

8va............................:

Op. 57.

&c.

&c.

As I have already pointed out, the opening of the last movement of the ninth symphony presented great difficulties: the solution reached in the 'Dona' of the Missa solemnis does not seem to me ideal, and Thayer (iv. 352) is of the same opinion. Perhaps it was impossible to get complete equalization here: on the other hand, we find balance of the two motives achieved in a quite similar case—i.e. in the Pastoral symphony.

Certain observations written between the sketches for this symphony, made in the year 1808, run as follows (N. II, p. 375):

'The audience must discover the situations for itself.'

'*Sinfonia caratteristica*—or reminiscences of life in the country.'

'A recollection of country life.'

'All pictures lose when carried too far in instrumental music.'

'*Sinfonia pastorella.* Any one who has preserved some idea of country life can imagine for himself, without any superscriptions, what the author intends.'

'Also he should be able to recognize the whole, without any description, since it has more emotional content than tone-painting.'

'Expression of gratitude. Lord, we thank Thee.'

These notes give us clearly the artistic experience; they fix the leading idea; they show, for instance in the fourth movement, the struggle between the expression and the artist's medium.

161. N. 80. p. 55.

In a sketch-book of the year 1803 Beethoven found a basic motive (Ex. 161), and the interesting note (Ex. 162) in the same sketch-book also belongs to the history of the original motives of the Pastoral symphony.

162. N. 80. p. 56.

Murmur of the streams

1mo.

The larger the stream the deeper the note

2do.

I consider that these examples clearly reveal the double foundation of Beethoven's music (as of all art) and the union of the two. They are both constructed by the imagination; but something further is required for the complete shaping of the work of art: and that is

(*c*) *Aesthetic judgement.*

Nottebohm has pointed out the active part played in Beethoven's compositions by the reflective intellect

(N. 80, p. 54). 'The alpha in Beethoven is imagination, and the omega is imagination, but it is an imagination permeated by reflection.' His remark, 'Reflection, however, is cold', aroused Riemann to contradict him; for Riemann considered it impossible (Riemann, p. 35) that 'anything can be effected by the interference of the aesthetic judgement, i.e. cautious, dispassionate intelligence'. But to put aesthetic judgement on a level with dispassionate intelligence is sheer perversity; the aesthetic judgement cannot be dealt with in terms of arithmetic. I should also like to object to Meumann's 'system' when he says that 'the elementary foundations of aesthetic enjoyment show a complete analogy with the elementary motives of artistic creation, since, in their very nature, aesthetic enjoyment and satisfaction can be no other than a feeling and understanding of what the artist has created' (p. 96). And when he goes on (p. 109) to set up as grades in the aesthetic attitude 'the purely sensuous', 'the aesthetico-critical' and 'the act of judging', it is clear that this aesthetic judgement does not correspond with the simple logical attitude, but inclines much more to that of artistic creation.

That Beethoven deliberately employed this judgement is testified by his words, 'I reject, and then try something fresh'. Still more clearly do we get this proof from the notes in his sketches, such as 'meilleur', 'besser', 'gut', and the like. And I do not doubt for a moment that in many cases he was fully aware of the fundamental inadequacy of the first plans; he knew better than any one else that in the sketch for the last movement of the A minor quartet Op. 132 (Ex. 6) the rhythm was too rigid and uniform. In due time, however, having discarded the first drafts as unsuitable, he discovered a form-idea adequate to express what he intended.

The sketches give us an opportunity of following in detail the continual alternation of actual artistic creation and aesthetic judgement. This dichotomy is to be found in the work of all artists. When Schubert [1] writes in his journal, 'My creative work has been brought about through grief plus musical understanding; those compositions created by grief alone seem to give least pleasure to the world', I seem to find in these words confirmation of my thesis. Busoni [2] gives a clear definition of the twofold character and the peculiar features of the aesthetic attitude: 'The composer can get just as much from one outpouring as a singer can sing in one breath. To carry this further, he has to link the parts together and add sequence, modulation, and contrast; also, unfortunately, he must intersperse it with conventional formulae. Test this before you contradict it. The apparently constructive process of developing a theme shown by the final reading requires as much inspiration as was needed for its first discovery. The moving force of this organism is the idea; the "regulator" is the instinct for proportion; the distributor of the content is the spirit; the bearer of the expression is the mind; the manufacturer is the ability.' And in his own peculiar way E. T. A. Hoffmann has defined this bipartition of the artist's work in 'Lichte Stunden eines wahnsinnigen Musikers, ein Buch für Kenner.'[3] 'Unconscious reception—the composer almost unconsciously arrives at definite knowledge—in this way he becomes his own critic—divided up into *two* mental principles, separated by the moment.'

And so perhaps we are dealing with a special peculiarity of Beethoven's creative process only in so far as here the two activities sometimes alternate markedly, and at other times are quite separate. Spitta (p. 181) says of Schubert: 'A great deal of his work came to him in the very act of writing', and of Händel: 'Composition and writing were almost simultaneous'; we may

[1] F. Schubert, *Die Dokumente seines Lebens, erste Hälfte*. Nr. 470, published by O. E. Deutsch.

[2] 'Der Bär', *Jahrbuch von Breitkopf und Härtel*, 1924, p. 92.

[3] *Musikalische Novellen*, published by E. Istel, p. 166.

assume that in these cases there can have been little of this alternation between creation and judgement. If the majority of composers share Beethoven's method of work, this explains why it is necessary to jot down the inspiration in writing. Which brings me to my last point—the importance of the sketches to Beethoven himself.

(d) *The importance of the sketches to Beethoven.*

Some of the sketches indubitably served as an aid to memory, in the sense indicated by Heuss. Riemann is certainly wrong when he says (p. 37): 'If we were to assume that the sketches represent what he first heard, we should get but a feeble idea of the composer's imaginative powers. These tenuous threads of melody and scraps of tune are to be regarded rather as intimations, intelligible to the composer alone, from a voice directing him from out a fully organic whole, complex and full of shading, which revived in his memory when he looked at the sketch.' This is in complete contradiction to the character of the sketches, their gradual, far-reaching development, and the critical notes inserted by Beethoven himself. And it is by no means certain that they were of such importance in aiding his memory, for we have many references to the strength of his powers in that direction. Amenda, Seyfried and Ries speak of the immediate repetition of free improvisations, of his playing a concertos without the help of a full solo-part, and his instantaneous detection of misprints in proof-reading. It is true that the memorizing of a whole piece is rather a different matter from remembering an isolated motive: and the conversation with Breuning quoted above (p. 147) shows that Beethoven himself was afraid of forgetting motives. I have frequently pointed out in the course of these remarks that Beethoven did actually take themes from the old sketch-books.

But the sketches had another value for him, a value

to which I have already referred. I have shown (Chap. III) how important this method of work was for the writing of his compositions, in view of the fact that he worked on several of these at a time. And even if Beethoven did say to Schlösser (Thayer, iv. p. 421): '. . . Because I sometimes work on several things at a time and still can depend on not confusing one with another', yet it must have been desirable, in the course of perpetual alteration and the changing of motives, to commit the intervening stages to writing. Spitta was obviously thinking of this when he wrote (p. 187): 'With this we can reconcile the fact that not only did a great many ideas come to him which at the time he did not develop further, but also that in the early stages of the developmental process he was very apt to lose the feeling of unity in his pre-occupation with detail, and was obliged to recapture it later by further effort.' Graf also discusses at some length this aspect of the importance of the sketches (p. 185 et seq.).

Actually, however, it is only the sketches for the motives and the larger fragments that come into question as aids to memory; their importance in rousing the feeling of unity arises only when we have to do with work carried out on several compositions at once. The sketches show not only these two aspects, but also a third, i.e. single bars and motives are more and more frequently taken up again, altered and remodelled. An instance of this is the theme for variations in Op. 127. Nottebohm (N. ii, p. 335 et seq.) brings together no less than nine experimental versions of the beginning of the song-cycle Op. 98 'Auf dem Hügel sitz' ich spähend in das blaue Nebelland', and as many as fifteen for the last four bars of the variations in the C sharp minor quartet Op. 131. Less extensive instances of the same kind are very frequent. Here there can be no question of the sketches having value merely as aids to memory or in the attempt towards unity. I shall now give my reasons for this opinion.

Beethoven had an extraordinarily lively imagination, but we should have no idea of its fertility if we merely considered his completed works. Schmitz [1] has calculated that, even if we take only the 'Beethoveniana' of Nottebohm into consideration, some thirty vocal and fifty instrumental compositions (and, among these, symphonies and sonatas) must have been set aside. Beethoven's creative imagination was never idle; as we have seen, it was unceasingly active, by night as well as by day, and whether he were at home or out of doors. It may well have interfered with his other work of giving shape to or altering his first ideas; and, to get the necessary peace for the exercise of this aesthetico-critical judgement, he required a handy vehicle, readily accessible to the senses. This was furnished by the written sketches. They forced his sense of touch, his sense of sight, and in the last instance, his imagination to proceed concentratedly in one direction; and so, by uniting the various motives of artistic creation, they made it possible to produce the ideal solution.

Whence come the original motives and ideas? This is the secret of genius, a secret of which the composer himself is unconscious. Beethoven's words to Schlösser (Thayer, iv. 421) are not very helpful. 'You will ask where I get my ideas from. I cannot say for certain. They come uncalled, sometimes independently, sometimes in association with other things. It seems to me that I could wrest them from Nature herself with my own hands as I go walking in the woods. They come to me in the silence of the night or in the early morning, stirred into being by moods which the poet would translate into words, but which I put into sounds; and these go through my head ringing and singing and storming until at last I have them before me as notes.' Some experience deposits, as it were, a precipitate, and this forms the foundation.

[1] Publications by the Beethoven House, Bonn, III, p. 10.

When Czerny [1] tells us that the E major adagio in the quartet Op. 59. 11 owes its origin to Beethoven's contemplation of the starry sky at night, we have here a concrete instance of this artistic experience.

The main form- and experience-motives can be established. The first part of this book was given up to this process, as must be any attempt to comprehend a personal style. It is also possible to discover the connexions which, in obedience to certain laws, are established between form and expression; in the second part, we attempted to trace some of these in the case of Beethoven. Schumann [2] says: 'All artistic effort is approximate', and, while this is undoubtedly true as regards the study of musical style, there seems no reason why we should not attempt to penetrate as deeply as we can into the personal idiosyncrasies. What is certain, however, is that an important part of what distinguishes the genius from his fellow-men must remain for ever miraculous and inexplicable.

What Schumann says is also true of the creative artist himself; he also must feel discouraged in the struggle we have described between the expression- and the form-motive. That there were such moments in Beethoven's life is shown by the poetical words quoted by J. A. Stumpff, words which are indubitably authentic, at least as regards their content (Thayer, v. 130): 'When at eventide I contemplate in wonderment the firmament and the host of luminous bodies which we call worlds and suns, eternally revolving within its boundaries, my spirit soars beyond these stars many millions of miles away towards the fountain whence all created work springs and whence all new creation must still flow. When from time to time I try to give shape and form in sound to the feelings roused within me, alas! I meet with cruel disappoint-

[1] F. Kerst, *Die Erinnerungen an Beethoven*, Bd. I, p. 53.
[2] Quoted from A. Schmitz, *Zeitschr. f. Musikwiss.*, Jahrgang 2, p. 537.

ment. In disgust I throw away the sheet of paper I have soiled, and am almost convinced that no earthborn being can ever hope to set down by means of sounds, words, colour, or in sculpture, the heavenly pictures that rise before his awakened imagination! What is to reach the heart must come from above: if it does not come thence, it will be nothing but notes—body without spirit. . . . The spirit must rise up from the earth, whence for a time the heavenly spark is banished. . . . For only by hard, persistent labour through such powers as are bestowed on a man can the work of art be made worthy of the Creator and Preserver of everlasting Nature.'

The sketches are witness to this 'hard, persistent labour'; and that Beethoven knew full well how to overcome his temporary doubt is shown by his immortal works.

VI

BEETHOVEN AS COMPOSER OF
INSTRUMENTAL MUSIC AND AS
WRITER OF SONGS

CERTAIN features in a composer's work are intimately
bound up with a definite intention to produce a mood:
these I shall call stylistic forms associated with expression. In their very nature, such forms are harder to
recognize than are those of the style determinants; our
task is made easier if we begin with a study of the vocal
music. Thus, in my work on the songs of Brahms [1]
I was able to demonstrate a large number of stylistic
features associated with musical expression.

With Beethoven the problem is much more difficult.
He knew that instrumental music was his chief
domain. Seyfried reports him as saying (Leitzmann,
p. 51): 'Although I know very well what my 'Fidelio' is
worth, yet I am equally certain that the symphony is my
real element. When I hear music within me, I am always listening to the full orchestra. I can demand anything of instrumentalists, but when I write for the voice
I have to keep asking myself, "Can that be sung?".'
And this reminds us of his exclamation, 'Does he suppose that I think of his wretched violin when the spirit
speaks to me?' (Spitta, p. 190). He is also reported
as saying to Rochlitz,[2] 'But Goethe now, *he* is a living
man, and we ought all to share his life with him. That
is why he lends himself to composition. There is no
one so adapted for composition as Goethe. Only I don't

[1] P. Mies, *Stilmomente und Ausdrucksstilformen im Brahms'schen
Lied,* 1923.

[2] From *Für Freunde der Tonkunst IV*, quoted from Friedländer.
Jahrbuch der Musikbibliothek Peters, 19. Jahrgang, p. 27.

really care for writing songs.' Schindler [1] tells us how obdurate Beethoven remained to the entreaties of singers, both men and women, in the matter of simplifying and lowering the vocal parts. We may question whether Schindler is right in thinking that 'it would have been quite easy for him, by changing the intervals here and there, to get rid of some of the vocal difficulties without making any essential change in the work itself'. For while the sketches for the instrumental works are numerous, those for the vocal works give the impression of still greater labour. In the second volume of Thayer's biography the sketch-book for 'Leonore' is discussed; eighteen different beginnings for Florestan's aria 'In des Lebens Frühlingstagen' and ten for the chorus 'Wer ein holdes Weib errungen' are mentioned (Thayer, ii. 466), and that does not include some that are illegible or only slightly altered. Moreover, Beethoven's habit of returning again and again to the same work, as in the course of composing the 'Ode an die Freude', the Song of Sacrifice, Matthison's song 'Wunsch', etc., is much less marked in the case of the instrumental music. There is the instance of the overture Op. 115, of course; but this is at times very closely bound up with the 'Ode to Joy' (N. 1, p. 41).

All the sketches show the extreme care with which Beethoven sought to follow the rhythmical structure and the emotional content of the text. Nottebohm adduces a number of sketches in which the melody is constructed on the metrical accentuation of the text, as, for instance, in the Song of Sacrifice (Ex. 163).

163. N. II. p. 542.

&c.

We shall find it interesting to consider here those cases in which this attempt to express the feeling coincides with the characteristic features in Beethoven's

[1] *Biographie von L. van Beethoven*, 1st ed. 1840, p. 154 et seq.

163

instrumental music with which I dealt in the first part of this book. 'Leonore' contains a false emphasis on the word 'dass' (Ex. 164 a); this does not occur in a sketch (Ex. 164 b), nor in the repetition of the same phrase four bars later in 'Leonore' (Ex. 164 c).

164 a. Prieger, p. 202.

O dass ich euch nicht loh - nen kann, nicht loh - nen kann

164 b. N. ii. p. 431.

O dass ich

164 c. Prieger, p. 202.

o mehr als ich er - tra - gen kann &c.

Possibly the series of short, sequential intervals, E→ A, G→D, following close on one another, may have been the reason in this case for bringing in a kind of sequence-contraction by prolongation of the A. The vocal impulse is reduced here by a 'formal' motive in the instrumental part. On the other hand, there are instances, of course, where the union of the two is perfectly effected. I have already quoted (Exs. 49 and 50) two places in 'Leonore' where the expression compelled a change in the melodic line and necessitated short sequences. The opening of Florestan's aria is another example of the same sort; here also the too short sequences in a number of the sketches had to undergo remodelling according to instrumental principles before complete unity of expression and form was achieved (Ex. 84).

A general survey makes it clear, however, that in the case of Beethoven it is difficult to set forth precisely the stylistic forms associated with expression. The following chapter may be regarded as an attempt to advance our present knowledge in some respects where evidence is furnished by the sketches.

164

VII

STYLE FEATURES ADOPTED FOR THEIR EXPRESSIVE VALUE

(a) The common chord and other structures in the melody.

I SHALL deal first of all with the common chord in melodic construction. Attention has already been drawn to the song 'Der freie Mann' (Ex. 149), the march from 'The Ruins of Athens' (Ex. 148), and the 'Dona nobis pacem' from the Missa solemnis (Ex. 150), together with the sketches for these. Here the common chord, frequently in descending form, is used along with a regularly measured tempo; all three compositions are characterized by pomp and solemnity. And we get this tempo again very often where the words express a mood of the kind: for instance, in Gellert's 'Die Himmel rühmen des Ewigen Ehre' (Op. 48. iv), in Goethe's 'Bundeslied' (Op. 122), and perhaps most strikingly in the two versions of Matthison's 'Opferlied' (Op. 121 b) for soprano with chorus and orchestral accompaniment, and for voice with pianoforte accompaniment. The sketches and drafts for the musical setting of this text extend over a period of many years (1794–1822); they all begin with the descending common chord, used in very even time to accord with the prosodic treatment (Ex. 163). It is clear from this that the thematic use of the common chord is definitely associated with the expression of solemnity.

It is possible to determine a number of other constant structures, though their limited number does not admit of our discovering definite style features adopted for their expressive value. The theme for the duet in 'Leonore', 'O namenlose Freude', was taken by Beethoven from the plan for an earlier opera; Ex. 165 a gives the form it had there, and we see that the libretto follows it freely. It should be noted that the first sketch to include this melody in 'Leonore' (Ex. 165 b) repro-

165

duces it without the words, in contrast to Florestan's part which immediately follows. It must be that in Beethoven's opinion its expression so exactly fitted in with the mood of the scene that he forced the unsuitable words on it in an unusual way (Ex. 165 c).

165 a.   N. I. p. 86.

Nie   war   ich   so   froh   wie heu - te

165 b.   N. II. p. 443.

&c.

Mein Weib, mein

165 c.   Prieger, p. 225.

O   na - men-, na - men - lo - se Freu - de!

He added a note to the beginning, even using repetition of notes so as to make it as little obvious as possible, and repeated two syllables of the text, which seem rather meaningless.

Now let us compare the following four passages:

(1) The theme of the 'Gegenliebe' by G. A. Bürger, from somewhere in the year 1794–5 (N. II, p. 535), which has as its textual climax 'dann, o Himmel, ausser sich, würde ganz mein Herz zerlodern!' (Ex. 166 a).

166 a.   Gegenliebe 1794–5.

dann, o Him - mel, aus - ser   sich, wür - de ganz mein Herz zer - lo - dern

(2) The text of the choral fantasy (from the year 1808) with the same melody, about where the following words occur:

> Grosses, das ins Herz gedrungen,
> Blüht dann neu und schön empor,

Hat ein Geist sich aufgeschwungen,
Hallt ihm stets ein Geisterchor.

Nehmt denn hin, ihr schönen Seelen,
Froh die Gaben schöner Kunst.
Wenn sich Lieb und Kraft vermählen,
Lohnt dem Menschen Götter-Gunst.

(3) An unused sketch, from the year 1804, for the chorus, 'Wer ein holdes Weib errungen' (Ex. 166 b).

166 b.   N. ii. p. 445.   1804.

(4) The theme for the ode in the ninth symphony, in the form given it in the sketch of 1822 (Ex. 166 c), which agrees with the final reading.

166 c.   N. ii. p. 165.   1822.

In these examples we see a consistent unity between the joyful mood of the text and the melodic line—a unity that is really astonishing when we consider the long period in Beethoven's life over which his work on this composition was distributed. It explains, moreover, how it is that in works from the most different periods the special features by means of which Beethoven expressed his emotion remain so clear and recognizable.

(*b*) *Suspension and descending seconds.*

Suspension and descending seconds are also employed in order to get the right expression. Here perhaps we are dealing with one of the most general connexions between motive and expression, common to all styles and to all periods;[1] to find it in Beethoven is therefore not surprising. It is interesting, however, to consider the development leading to motives and expression

[1] Cf. A. Molnar's observations, *Zeitschrift für Musikwissenchaft*, Jahrgang V, p. 414.

of this kind. The object is to give voice to something tender, elegiac and wistful. The tenderness in the suspensions in the theme of the Spring sonata Op. 24 (Exs. 53 and 39) and the sighing of the descending seconds in Florestan's aria (Ex. 84) have already been discussed, together with their development. We find another example when we compare the sketch for the 'Wonne der Wehmut' and its final form. As is so often the case with vocal compositions, the sketches do not begin with the opening words, but with passages from the middle of the song. The final reading (Ex. 167 b) replaces the broken line of the sketch by consistent suspensions and descending seconds, and this very much helps out the expression of melancholy.

167 a.   N. ii. p. 281.

Ach,   nur dem halb - ge-trock - ne - ten Au - ge   wie ö - de   wie

todt

167 b.   Op. 83. 1.

Ach,   nur dem halb - ge-trock-ne-ten Au - ge wie ö - de,   wie

sf

todt   die Welt ihm er - scheint

sf   sf   sf   dim.   p

Here we may also consider two passages from 'Leonore'. I have already mentioned that the motive for the words in 'Leonore' 'Ihr sollt ja nicht zu klagen haben' (Ex. 137 b) originally belonged to Rocco's part (Ex. 137 d). It is not mere chance that we find a difference between the two cadences, for in a further series of sketches the repetitions in Rocco's part in the conclusion are written as in the final form (Ex. 137 a). And the grace-notes to the words 'trag' ich es immer schon bei mir' (Ex. 168) accentuate this expression of grief.

168. Prieger, p. 197.

trag' ich es im - mer schon bei mir

In all these examples the words tell us what the composer's intention must have been with regard to the musical expression; but the sketches also give us direct evidence. We find one instance in the conclusion to the Missa solemnis: the sketch (Ex. 169 a) contains descending seconds—actual sighs, as it were—and the note alongside, 'throughout simple prayer, prayer, prayer', makes Beethoven's intention still clearer. In the final form (Ex. 169 b) the seconds are harmonized —an example of 'absolute' melody. Finally, there has been preserved an unused sketch for the second movement of Op. 181, the note accompanying which, 'les derniers soupirs', gives support to Amenda's statement that the burial scene from 'Romeo and Juliet' was the idea giving shape to the movement.

169 a. N. II. p. 465.

pa • • - •cem

169 b. Missa solemnis.

pa - cem pa - cem

170. N. II. p. 485.
les derniers soupirs.

How much more successful is the final reading than
is the mere 'tone-painting' of the sketch! And the poetical idea cannot have counted with the composer for
anything very essential, since he suppressed every hint
of it. Even if Beethoven did once say to Schindler [1]
that 'the period in which he wrote his sonatas was more
poetical than the present (1823), and consequently
indications of this sort were at that time superfluous',
still even at a later date he gives us these hints only very
seldom.

(c) 'Ornament'.

In the first part of this book [Chap. I (b)] I pointed
out the importance of a certain 'ornament' as regards
the melodic line and the melodic apex. In the case of
Brahms [2] I have shown the close connexion that exists
between ornament and musical expression. Though in
a lesser degree, the sketches give us some clues to the
importance of other ornaments in Beethoven's music
also. Ex. 55 gave a sketch and the final form of the
theme of Op. 18. II. In the intervening sketch (Ex. 171)
the final rhythm is already shown; but only with the

[1] *Biographie von L. van Beethoven*, 1st ed., p. 198.
[2] Op. cit., p. 117 et seq.

introduction of the grace-note do we get the effect of perfect elegance.

171. N. II. p. 485.

The sketches for the beginning of the minuet in the sonata Op. 22 (Exs. 138 a, b, and c) show how much more graceful the melodic line has become in the final reading, an effect to which the grace-note largely contributes. Greater difficulty attended the filling-out of the similar line in the quartet Op. 18. IV (Ex. 138 b). And this figure which appears in the sonata frequently occurs where it is a question of minuet-like, elegant, 'scherzoso' movements; we find it, for instance, when the theme returns in the first movement 'in tempo d'un menuetto' in the sonata Op. 54 (Ex. 172), and in a theme of the 'andante con moto, ma non troppo, poco scherzoso' in the quartet Op. 130 (Ex. 173).

172. Op. 54.

&c.

173. Op. 130.

I may also mention, though without quoting the actual notes, the second theme of the 'andante scherzoso, più allegretto' from the violin sonata Op. 23, the rondo theme 'allegretto' from the sonata Op. 31. I, the second theme of the 'allegro piacevole' from the violin sonata Op. 12. II,[1] and the scherzo trio from the violin sonata Op. 96. If we consider it from this point of view, we can readily understand the change in the writing of the minuet in Op. 59. III (Ex. 132). Originally the theme had this figure in the first bar (Ex. 132 a), and the viola reproduced it in the trio (Ex. 132 b); but

[1] *Piacevole* = charming and graceful. (Riemann, *Musiklexikon.*)

while the line of the minuet became more flowing, the trio became more hard and set: and the elegant figure, being no longer in keeping there, was changed for something more solid (Ex. 132 d). We may therefore regard this use of the grace-note in medium tempo as the stylistic form connected with the expression of elegance and grace.

A few examples from the vocal music will serve to support this view. One is taken from 'Adelaide' (Ex. 174), another from the song 'Feuerfarb' (Ex. 175), and a third from 'Neue Liebe, neues Leben' (Ex. 176): all three have the same light and graceful character.

174. Adelaide.

A - bend - lüft - chen im zar - ten Lau - be flü - stern

175. Feuerfarb.

Die ach - te ich hö - her als Sil - ber und Gold

Pianoforte.

176. Neue Liebe, neues Leben.

Weg ist al - les was du lieb - test, weg wa - rum du dich be - trüb - test

Pianoforte.

A second kind of ornament behind which lies an obvious intention in musical expression differs very little as regards the notes themselves from the one I have just discussed; the essential feature is its quicker tempo. A sketch for the trio Op. 1. 11 forms the avenue of approach to this stylistic form. In Ex. 177 a it is evident that Beethoven's object was to give very definite

172

shape to the second and fourth bars; but this brought
about an unnatural restlessness. The final form avoids
this (Ex. 177 b), but retains the clear definition by
means of the grace-note.

Other examples are the scherzo theme of the sonata
Op. 30. II (Ex. 178) and a presto theme from the
quartet Op. 130 (Ex. 179).

It is characteristic of this use of the grace-note that it
is frequently accompanied by dynamic effects, i.e. strong
crescendi, *fp*, *sf*, either occurring simultaneously with it
(as in Ex. 179), or very near to it (Ex. 178). I may also
mention the grace-note which is an essential part of the
melody in Op. 18. VI (Ex. 180); it is true that here we
have to do with a long appoggiatura [1], but the quick
tempo, allegro con brio ₵, gives the necessary sharpness of definition.

[1] A. Beyschlag, *Die Ornamentik der Musik*, p. 215.

173

Further examples are to be found in the finale of Op. 127, in the beginning of Op. 18. v (Ex. 54), and in the finale of Op. 18. iv: in every case the dynamic effects are always close to the grace-note. The intention is to make the music clear-cut and effective. And here, in comparing these two stylistic forms in musical expression, so often similar in external features, we recognize the importance of dynamics and of tempo.

In the foregoing I have done no more than give a slight introduction to a study of the importance of ornament to musical expression. I believe that ornament and melism have a special function in this respect, and that the term 'ornament' is in most cases misleading. Removal of these ornaments would not only rob the melody of decoration, but frequently would completely alter the expression. We have here a field that will well repay further investigation.

(d) 'Character' of the keys.

The 'character' of keys is a problem that has been much debated, but is still quite unsolved. It has always been maintained, however, that Beethoven was a supporter of the theory that the various keys have different characters. Schindler (N. ii, p. 326) states that Beethoven agreed in the main with the theory advanced by C. F. D. Schubart, but did not share all that author's views. As a matter of fact, some scattered remarks of Beethoven's have come down to us that seem to bear this out. H. Stephani [1] quotes him as saying that 'the central point of the key system may have its own place, though this is not fixed and immovable. Hence, he was capable of recognizing every key, the mood being whichever it chooses.' Concerning Klopstock he said to Rochlitz, 'He always begins far too high up above his audience. With him it is always *maestoso!* D flat major! Isn't that so?' And in his sketches we find at

---

[1] *Der Stimmungscharakter der Tonarten*, p. 4.

one place the observation 'B minor, black key' (N. 11, p. 326).

It is of very great interest, therefore, to bring together what the sketches reveal concerning the keys and the changes introduced with regard to them. We find, namely, that Beethoven frequently changed his mind about the key, though less often in the vocal works than in the instrumental. I have already referred to the fixed plan for the modulation in 'Leonore' (p. 140). With one exception, the numerous beginnings for the song 'Die Sehnsucht' (Die stille Nacht umdunkelt) are written in E major; and this key is also used in the sketches for the 'Opferlied', though these cover a number of years, and in the two final readings.

I shall attempt to assemble these key-changes in groups, arranged according to the reasons that presumably induced them. Firstly, we may be dealing with the interpolation of a theme into a cyclical work of which the main key is already determined. Thus, the rondo of the violin sonata Op. 24 was originally sketched in F sharp major (Ex. 98, in which the key signature is incomplete; we must imagine the addition of two sharps), and only later on was it transposed into F major: the form apparently was responsible for this, but nevertheless it is a conspicuous change of key. The andante in F major belonging to the sonata Op. 53 was at first sketched in E major (N. 80, p. 61), and the melodic structure was in part different. The trio for the sixth symphony, which was taken over from an old note-book, was written in B flat (Ex. 161), whereas now it is in F major . And the theme of the sonatina Op. 79 in G major was first sketched in the sub-dominant key C major (Ex. 104). The second theme of the slow movement of the ninth symphony was in A major instead of in D major (Ex. 18), and the oft-quoted finale theme of the A minor quartet Op. 132 was originally in D minor (Exs. 6 and 73), having been conceived as the last movement for the ninth symphony. It would have fitted in not badly with the tragic quality of the key of D minor in Beethoven's music, of which Gal (p. 86) speaks. In all these last instances we are dealing with keys separated by fifths and thus closely related to one another. It is another matter when we come to the alla danza tedesca of Op. 130. Originally it was written in A major and destined for the A minor quartet; when it was embodied in the B flat major quartet, it was changed to B flat major, and finally it was altered to G major (Ex. 59). The following brings together the keys of the quartet movements of Op. 130 as they appear in the final form.

Movement	I	II	III	IV	V	VI
Key	B flat major	B flat minor	D flat major	G major	E flat major	B flat major
Harmonic function	T	∘T	∘Tp	Variant of Tp	S	T

This sort of key-construction seems extraordinarily rich. First there is the move away from the tonic to the tonic and parallel circles, and then the building up from the sub-dominant; to use B flat major for the fourth movement would have interrupted this development. A similar relation comes to mind, which Nottebohm (N. ii. p. 206) demonstrated in the Bagatelles Op. 126 —i.e. the relation between the keys in thirds, the importance of which in the case of Beethoven has already been abundantly referred to in the literature.

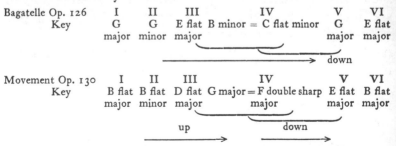

In this way the cyclical string quartet is compelled to return to the original key.

176

The pianoforte sonata in E major Op. 14. 1 was transformed by Beethoven himself into a string quartet in the key of F major; since ♮ occurs frequently in the pianoforte bass, the reason for the transposition must have been to use ♮, accessible to the violoncello. And Beethoven himself entrusted to his publisher an arrangement of the E flat septet Op. 20 for flute, violin, two violas, and violoncello, transposed to G major, possibly also on account of the greater simplicity of this key when written (Thayer, ii. p. 239). The minuet in Op. 59. III was originally written in F major (Ex. 88 b), the trio in D flat major; in a later sketch (N. 11, p. 89) the second part of the trio begins in A flat major. The final form is in C major and F major. Possibly neither D flat nor A flat major were suitable keys for getting the required sharpness with the string instruments: the figure underwent a similar change in the case of the violas (pp. 106, 152). It may be that the quality of the tone counted for something in this; certainly this seems to be the case with the adagio of the sonata Op. 30. II. Originally it was written in G major, later on in A flat major (Ex. 101); both keys are adapted to the cyclical form, the one as the dominant, the other as standing a third from the main key. G major, however, was too light a key for this melancholy mood, especially in the case of the violin, on account of the open strings. We therefore get the converse of the foregoing:

Movement		I	II	III	IV
Key	Sketch	C minor	G major	C major	C minor
	Final form	C minor	A flat major	C major	C minor

In the last examples use was made of the different tone-colour of the keys on the string instruments. The instances given earlier are instructive, in which the same line pursues a different development. A sketch in E flat major has been found (Ex. 138) which is the nucleus of the C minor scherzo of Op. 18. iv and of the B flat major minuet of Op. 22. The filling out of the line follows a mood of pathos and passion, and tends in the direction of C minor, a key which very often has this character in Beethoven's compositions (Gal, p. 86, fifth symphony, funeral cantata, &c.). If, on the other hand, the movement of the sonata Op. 22 had remained in E flat major, the contrast with the slow movement, which is also in that key, would have been too slight. Moreover, E flat major appears frequently as the key denoting something elegant and tender. A passage from a letter to Thomson concerning the Scottish songs treated by Beethoven runs as follows (Thayer, iii. 373)—'The two last songs in your letter of the 21st December pleased me very much. I have therefore written the music for them con amore, more especially for the second of the two. You have written it in 🎼,

but I consider this neither natural enough nor appropriate to the superscription "amoroso", it turns it rather into "barbaresco"; accordingly I have put the song into the key that is really suitable for it.' In series 24 of the collected works are the settings of Scottish and other songs, and, among these, twenty in which the word 'amoroso' occurs in the tempo specification. Six of these are in E flat major, five in D major, three in F major, two in C major; and of the others, there is one in each of the following keys—B flat major, G minor, C minor, and B minor; clearly, E flat major and D major are the favourites. The sketch for the song Op. 108. xi is in F major, but the final form is written in E flat major (N. 11, p. 327); and here also we are dealing with a love-song. The reason for this change cannot be the high range of the voice part, as we see by comparing this song with the others in the same opus. The march with chorus from the 'Ruins of Athens'

178

shows vacillation between D major and E flat major; first it is written in D, later on in E flat. It is really a case here of a ceremonial occasion.[1] The part for the maidens, who perform graceful dances to the words 'Pflücket die Rosen, Schmückt die Altäre', may have induced Beethoven to employ the key of E flat major. Three of the four versions of Goethe's 'Sehnsucht' are in G minor, the third is in E flat major. In the middle part of it G minor also appears, and, in the second strophe of the fourth, E flat major. There are also sketches[2] for these songs in G minor. And the one version of the Italian aria 'l'amante impaziente' (Op. 82. iii) with the sub-title 'arietta buffa' is in E flat major, while the 'arietta assai seriosa' to the same Italian text (Op. 82. iv) is in B flat major. The German translation, which appeared at the same time with the publication of the original, calls the first 'Stille Frage', and the second 'Liebes-Ungeduld', which clearly indicates that the character of the first is intended to be graceful and tender. I may also mention the E flat major septet Op. 20, which, on the whole, has the same atmosphere.

On the other hand, E flat major may be used to impart a certain solemn character, as is shown by the pianoforte concerto in that key, Op. 73, and by the 'Ruins of Athens' already mentioned. Solemnity of the themes in notes of the common chord helps to this effect (p. 146); both these stylistic forms produce the same musical expression. The slow movement of the concerto Op. 73 was first written in C major (Ex. 142 b); as the rhythms were polished, the key changed to B flat major. The reverse process occurred with the march that took origin from the same rhythmical motive: it was transposed into F major (Ex. 142 c) from E flat major (Ex. 142 d), which,

[1] Above the words of the chorus Kotzebue writes 'Wechselgesang der Priester und Jungfrauen' (N. ii, p. 141).
[2] G. Kinsky, *Katalog des Musikhistorischen Museums von W. Heyer in Köln*, Bd. IV, p. 164.

as I have been maintaining, is the key suited to a march rhythm. This is rather rare, for the keys Beethoven specially preferred for march music were E flat, D and C major, as is shown by the following:

E flat major: Op. 45. II for pianoforte (four hands); Op. 91, marcia 'Rule Britannia'; Op. 113, march with chorus from the 'Ruins'.

D major: Op. 8, march from the serenade; Op. 25, entrada from the serenade; Op. 43, march from 'Die Geschöpfe des Prometheus'; Op. 45. III for pianoforte (four hands), military march in D major.

C major: Op. 45. I for pianoforte (four hands); Op. 89, polonaise for pianoforte; Op. 91, marcia 'Marlborough', triumphal march for 'Tarpeja'.

F major: Op. 101, in the manner of a march, for military music.

It may also be mentioned here that in the scheme for modulation in 'Leonore' already quoted the key E flat major is introduced at the words 'Wir müssen gleich zum Werke schreiten'. The passage is characterized by a certain solemnity; note also the thematization on the common chord. Summarizing, therefore, we may say that in Beethoven's music the key of E flat major is introduced in association with moods denoting ceremonial or else tenderness and grace.

C major is the key of joy. We can see this in the C major marches and in the themes brought together in Ex. 166 for the 'Gegenliebe', in the choral fantasy, and in the sketch for 'Wer ein holdes Weib errungen'. Although the melodic construction is quite different, this chorus remains in C major in 'Leonore'. It is characteristic, moreover, that the overture Op. 115 was first sketched in E flat major, and then in G major (Ex. 114); but as soon as Schiller's ode became associated with the music (N. 1, p. 41) it appeared in C major, and in that key it finally remained. The writing of the ode to joy in D major in the ninth symphony is due to considerations of form: yet, when all is said and done, this key also belongs to the same musical mood, as the sketches for the 'Ruins' (Ex. 148) and the marches in D major attest. Finally, we have two direct indications of the spirit of gaiety that Beethoven attached to C major. On p. 152 I mentioned that in the sketches for the melancholy A flat major theme of Op. 127 there is suddenly introduced a merry variation in C major, while a fragment still connected with this bears the superscription 'la gaieté'. Another sketch, for piano,[1] brings together two pieces above which appear the words 'lustig' and 'traurig'; the first is in C major, the second in C minor.

As a final example I shall take the re-instrumentation of the A flat minor funeral march from the A flat major sonata, Op. 26, written for string instruments, two flutes, two clarinets in A, two bassoons, two horns in D, two horns in E, and kettle-drums. This march was intended for a drama by Duncker, and was written in B minor (N. 11, p. 324). It would have been a good example of the 'black' key.

The foregoing groupings, depending as they do, not on aesthetic assessment of the 'moods' they reflect, but rather on the superscriptions, the author's notes as to the mood intended, and the alterations in the sketches, make it probable that for Beethoven the various keys had definite emotional values that caused him to prefer certain of them to illustrate certain states of mind. I have proved this, to some extent, for the keys E flat major, C major, and D major, and I have indicated that something of the same kind also holds good for A flat major, F major, and B minor. At the same time, I think there is justice in Hennig's observation [2] that 'in my personal experience, the character of a key is brought out only when there are suitable harmonies, i.e. harmonies belonging to the key and sufficiently rich to

[1] Collected works, Series XXV, no. 37.
[2] R. Hennig, *Die Charakteristik der Tonarten*, 1896, p. 71.

sustain its effect'. As a matter of fact, in all the examples I have quoted, we have to do with a very definite tonality. I have likewise pointed out that Beethoven also interchanged very distantly related keys (such as F sharp and F, A, G, and B flat), but chiefly for reasons connected with the form.

(e) Notation and musical expression.

Gal (p. 106) has brought together some themes with long note-values. Concerning these he says: 'The principal contrast of the second theme always results from the rhythmical structure. When the principal theme introduces lively rhythms, the second theme is usually kept very steady by means of long values.' He gives examples from the sextet Op. 71, the septet Op. 20, the 'Pathetic' sonata Op. 13, the quartet Op. 18. iv and the scherzo of the quartet Op. 95. In these we deal, for the most part, with episodic themes from lively rondo or finale movements. Now the sketches show that in the final form the themes, though in other respects quite like the original, have different note-values. The possible changes fall into two groups—(1) those in which the note-values of the sketch have been halved in the final form, and (2) those in which they have been doubled.

The curious thing is that this logical dichotomy has an actual counterpart in the form. The halving of note-value is introduced in the first themes of quick movements and in those andante movements in which the tempo indicated is con moto or something similar. The doubling takes place in slow movements and in the episodic themes of quick movements. The latter case takes us back to Gal's themes. I give examples of the two groups.

1. *Halving the note-value of the sketch.* The principal theme of the overture Op. 115, allegro assai vivace (Ex. 114), and the first theme of the finale in the trio,

Op. 1. II presto (Ex. 25). We can see why the second theme in the latter must also be halved. (Ex. 181.)

181. N. II. p. 25.

Presto.

Op. 1. II.

The first theme of the rondo in the pianoforte concerto Op. 15, allegro scherzando; for according to a sketch its conclusion is written in quavers and not in semiquavers as in the final form. The first theme of the presto in the string trio Op. 9. 1 (N. II, p. 43); the allegro molto, quasi presto of Op. 18. II (N. II, p. 60); the theme of the slow movement of the fifth symphony (Ex. 90), andante con moto; the first theme of the andante in F major for pianoforte, which at first was written with the same note-values as in the final form, but went through an intermediate stage, andante grazioso con moto, in which these were doubled.

2. *Doubling the note-value of the sketch.* The second theme of the prestissimo finale in the trio Op. 1. III (Ex. 182): in this case the value is actually quadrupled.

182. N. II. p. 26.

&c.

Op. 1. III.

&c.

The first theme of the tempo di minuetto ma molto moderato e grazioso in the sonata Op. 30. III. In the first sketch (Ex. 27) the note-value is as in the final reading; between the writing of the first sketch and of the final form, Beethoven temporarily halved it, and then afterwards doubled it again. The largo in the pianoforte concerto Op. 15 (N. II, p. 65); the slow movement of the ninth symphony (Ex. 113), adagio molto e cantabile.

It would appear, therefore, that Beethoven considered the purely optical impression important. For him the feeling of rest was associated with long notes, and movement with short. Conversely, he tried to convey the intended expression by the character of the notation. We may further convince ourselves of this by two examples from the vocal music. The notation in the sketch for Clärchen's song 'Die Trommel gerühret' (Ex. 183 a) does not give us the impression of a march-like rhythm in the way that the final form does (Ex. 183 b).

183 a. N. II. p. 277.

Die Trom-mel ge-rüh-ret

183 b. Op. 84. I.
Vivace.

Die Trom - mel ge - rüh - ret

And the 'et ascendit' of the sketch (Ex. 184 a) is totally lacking in the force given by the notation of the final reading (Ex. 184 b) with the direction allegro molto ¢.

184 a. N. II. p. 149.

et a - scen - dit

&c.

184 b. Op. 123.
Allegro molto.

et a - scen - - -

&c.

There are only a few instances of departure from this general law. The sketch for the allegro molto e vivace from Sonata Op. 27. I is in 6/8, whereas the final form is in 3/4 time (Ex. 185).

Op. 27. 1.
Allegro molto e vivace.

In this case we are dealing with a C-type in sixteen simple or eight double bars; the up-beat shown in the sketch is actually dropped out. But the 3/8 time made the music look too 'short-winded'; so these rapid notes were equalized with the slower ones of the interlude. The other example is the slow movement in the Eroica (Exs. 145 and 56). The first sketch, which is far removed from the final form, shows the doubled note-value; the marked rhythm of the Marcia funebre does not make any striking impression on the eye. As in Clärchen's song (Ex. 183), the crotchet becomes a minim. With all this before us, we can now understand the alteration of the note-value when the last movement of the octet Op. 103 was remodelled for the quintet Op. 4 (cf. p. 55).

186 a. Octet Op. 103.
Finale. *Presto.*

Clarinet.

&c.

&c.

186 b. Quintet Op. 4.
Finale. *Presto.*

Violin.

&c.

&c.

In the octet the eye detects no great difference between the first theme and the second (Ex. 186 a); the halving of the note-value takes place in the quintet mainly in consequence of the lively character of the first theme in that composition (Ex. 186 b). It seems to me that, purely from the optical standpoint, the difference is greatly increased; at the same time, observe that the first bars of the second theme still retain their original length.

From this we may confidently affirm that for Beethoven even the aspect of a theme was of importance. This conclusion gives further support to an opinion which I advanced on p. 159, i.e. that the sketches owe their origin, in large part, to the fact that Beethoven liked to visualize his works, and perhaps was psychologically dependent on so doing. Here also, therefore, expression and form—even external form—are very clearly associated (cf. p. 69).

CONCLUSION

Our critical comparison of the sketches and the final forms has yielded us a considerable number of style determinants in the melodic line of Beethoven, the form of his melody, and the unity of his whole work: it has demonstrated a number of stylistic forms associated with musical expression, and has opened up the possibility of getting a general insight into Beethoven's creative methods. This forms the starting-point for further investigation. First we must study all these style determinants in the collected works, considering more especially, for instance, how far the type of the theme is dependent on its position (as first or second theme in the movement of a sonata, as theme for variations, etc.). The principles underlying the working-out must be investigated by extending our study of the sketch-books, such as that for the Eroica (N. 80), where much valuable material is to be found. Of this note-book Graf (p. 206) says: 'The study of the Eroica sketches shows us with what precision Beethoven balanced the several parts of the symphony; we see how the growth of one section is directly followed by increase in an adjoining section; the changing of one part involves that of another, and the later portions of the work develop out of the earlier.' Schmitz has already contributed something germane to this question in his principle of 'contrasting derivation'. But so long as nothing has been published corresponding to N. 80 this line of research, based as it must be on the original sketch-books, presents special difficulties.

I also think it not unprofitable to continue the search for more of the style features associated with musical expression. I consider that much of the so-called 'ornament' is of great importance from this point of view.

Or again, let me remark that in the present book I have scarcely touched on the question of harmonic structure, since my material has been drawn from sketches, which are mostly written for one part.

Another line of study, and one very important for our knowledge of the artist's development, might be concerned with the change during the course of the composer's life in the style determinants and style features whose object is expression. And finally, we ought to compare all the peculiarities of Beethoven's style with those of contemporary masters, and more especially Haydn, Mozart, and Schubert. Here and there I have touched on this point briefly, but to work out the comparison fully is beyond the scope of the present book.

Spitta concluded his review of Nottebohm's 'Beethoveniana' with these words (p. 195)—'It is clear that the source here opened up is going to be of supreme importance for research concerning Beethoven throughout the coming epoch.' In the historico-chronological direction the sketch-books have been used by Nottebohm and the revisers of Thayer's work; whereas on the side concerned with the study of style they have scarcely been exploited at all, if we except a few points in Riemann, Gal, and Becking. And yet it seems to me that this second value of theirs is the one of greater importance, for only so do they become material for constructing the 'inner history' (p. 1) of the master.

LIST OF ABBREVIATIONS

Song type = S type. 8-bar (16-bar, &c.) S type = S8, S16, &c.

Continuation type = C type.

Song type, the several parts of which are of the C type = S(C) type.

Continuation type, the several parts of which are of the S type = C(S) type.

In indicating the plan on which the theme is constructed,   ‖:   :‖ means repetition of a motive, and X means sequence of a motive.

BIBLIOGRAPHY

G. Becking, Studien zu Beethovens Personalstil. Das Scherzothema, 1921. = Becking

L. van Beethoven, Leonore, Oper in drei Akten. Klavierauszug, herausgegeben von E. Prieger, 1905. = Prieger

W. Fischer, Zur Entwicklungsgeschichte des Wiener klassischen Stils. Wiener Studien zur Musikwissenschaft III, 1915. = Fischer

H. Gal, Die Stileigentümlichkeiten des jungen Beethoven. Wiener Studien zur Musikwissenschaft IV, 1916. = Gal

M. Graf, Die innere Werkstatt des Musikers, 1910. = Graf

A. Heuss, Beethoven in der jüngsten Gegenwart. Zeitschr. f. Musikwiss. III. Jahrg., 1920/21. = Heuss

H. Jalowetz, Beethovens Jugendwerke in ihren melodischen Beziehungen zu Mozart, Haydn und C. Ph. E. Bach; Sammelb. d. IMG., XII. Jahrg. 1910/11. = Jalowetz

A. Leitzmann, L. van Beethoven. Berichte der Zeitgenossen, Briefe und persönliche Aufzeichnungen. 2 Bände, 1921. = Leitzmann

E. Meumann, System der Ästhetik, 3. Aufl., 1919 = Meumann

G. Nottebohm, Beethoveniana, Aufsätze und Mitteilungen, 1872. = N.I

= = Zweite Beethoveniana, nachgelassene Aufsätze, 1887. = N.II

G. Nottebohm, Ein Skizzenbuch von Beethoven
aus dem Jahre 1803. In Auszügen dargestellt,
1880.[1]   = N.80

= = Ein Skizzenbuch von Beethoven. Beschrieben
und in Auszügen dargestellt, 1865.[1]   = N.65

H. Riemann, Spontane Phantasietätigkeit und ver-
standesmässige Arbeit in der tonkünstlerischen
Produktion. Jahrbuch der Musikbibliothek
Peters, XVI. Jahrg., 1909.   = Riemann

A. Schmitz, Beethovens zwei Prinzipe. Ihre Be-
deutung für Themen und Satzbau, 1923.   = Schmitz

Ph. Spitta, 'Beethoveniana', in 'Zur Musik', 16
Aufsätze, 1892.   = Spitta

Thayer-Deiters-Riemann, L. van Beethovens
Leben, I[3] 1917, II[2] 1910, III[2] 1911, IV 1907,
V 1908.   = Thayer I—V

[1] New edition in one volume with preface by P. Mies, 1924.

LIST OF WORKS CITED

Op.

1. II. Trio für Pianoforte, Violine und Violoncell, 20, 183.

1. III. Trio für Pianoforte, Violine und Violoncell, 31, 75, 183.

2. I. Sonate für Pianoforte, 107, 139.

2. II. Sonate für Pianoforte, 49, 107.

2. III. Sonate für Pianoforte, 33, 111.

4. Quintett für 2 Violinen, 2 Bratschen und Violoncell, 55, 186.

7. Sonate für Pianoforte, 50.

8. Serenade für Violine, Bratsche und Violoncell, 12, 54, 180.

9. I Trio für Violine, Bratsche und Violoncell, 183.

9. II. Trio für Violine, Bratsche und Violoncell, 12.

10. I. Sonate für Pianoforte, 48.

10. II. Sonate für Pianoforte, 49, 108, 111.

10. III. Sonate für Pianoforte, 11, 41, 117.

11. Trio für Pianoforte, Klarinette und Violoncell, 89.

12. II. Sonate für Pianoforte und Violine, 171.

13. Sonate für Pianoforte, 32, 182.

14. I. Sonate für Pianoforte, 115, 119, 177.

18. I. Quartett für 2 Violinen, Bratsche und Violoncell, 119, 177.

14. II. Sonate für Pianoforte, 47, 62.

15. Konzert für Pianoforte mit Begleitung des Orchesters, 64, 184.

16. Quintett für Pianoforte, Oboe, Klarinette, Horn und Fagott, 23, 28, 30.

18. I. Quartett für 2 Violinen, Bratsche und Violoncell, 34, 46, 59, 93, 109, 125, 170.

18. II. Quartett für 2 Violinen, Bratsche und Violoncell, 38, 96, 101, 125, 171, 183.

18. III. Quartett für 2 Violinen, Bratsche und Violoncell, 18, 109, 153.

18. IV. Quartett für 2 Violinen, Bratsche und Violoncell, 32, 123, 171, 178, 182.

18. V. Quartett für 2 Violinen, Bratsche und Violoncell, 10, 27, 37, 57, 88, 102, 174.

18. VI. Quartett für 2 Violinen, Bratsche und Violoncell, 70, 82, 119, 152, 174.

Op.

19.　　　Konzert für Pianoforte mit Begleitung des Orchesters, 118.

20.　　　Septett für Violine, Bratsche, Horn, Klarinette, Fagott, Violoncell und Kontrabass, 177, 179, 182.

22.　　　Sonate für Pianoforte, 6, 9, 17, 37, 41, 124, 171, 178.

23.　　　Sonate für Pianoforte und Violine, 171.

24.　　　Sonate für Pianoforte und Violine, 17, 28, 37, 82, 124, 168, 175.

25.　　　Serenade für Flöte, Violine und Bratsche, 180.

26.　　　Sonate für Pianoforte, 78, 181.

27. I.　　Sonate für Pianoforte, 9, 17, 184.

27. II.　　Sonate für Pianoforte, 108.

28.　　　Sonate für Pianoforte, 108.

30. I.　　Sonate für Pianoforte und Violine, 54, 106, 130.

30. II.　　Sonate für Pianoforte und Violine, 14, 86, 88, 173, 177.

30. III.　Sonate für Pianoforte und Violine, 12, 22, 128, 140, 183.

31. I.　　Sonate für Pianoforte, 171.

31. III.　Sonate für Pianoforte, 109.

36.　　　II. Symphonie, 69, 117.

43.　　　Die Geschöpfe des Prometheus, 180.

45.　　　3 Märsche für das Pianoforte zu 4 Händen, 57, 59, 127, 180.

46.　　　'Adelaide', für 1 Singstimme mit Begleitung des Pianoforte, 12, 172.

47.　　　Sonate für Pianoforte und Violine, 129.

48. IV.　Die Ehre Gottes in der Natur, 165.

49. II.　　Sonate für Pianoforte, 23, 25.

51. II.　　Rondo für Pianoforte, 125.

52. II.　　'Feuerfarb'', Lied für 1 Singstimme mit Begleitung des Pianoforte, 172.

53.　　　Sonate für Pianoforte, 11, 17, 31, 128, 141, 175.

54.　　　Sonate für Pianoforte, 171.

55.　　　III. Symphonie (Eroica), 13, 40, 57, 61, 70, 84, 127, 134, 139, 141, 143, 185, 187.

57.　　　Sonate für Pianoforte, 80, 142, 153.

58.　　　Konzert für Pianoforte mit Begleitung des Orchesters, 126.

59. I.　　Quartett für 2 Violinen, Bratsche und Violoncell, 37, 40, 63, 106.

59. II.　　Quartett für 2 Violinen, Bratsche und Violoncell, 18, 19, 24, 64, 160.

Op.

59. III. Quartett für 2 Violinen, Bratsche und Violoncell, 73, 79, 109, 171, 177.

62. Ouvertüre zu 'Coriolan', 46.

67. V. Symphonie, 22, 39, 56, 75, 90, 128, 178, 183.

68. VI. Symphonie (Pastorale), 149, 153.

69. Sonate für Pianoforte und Violoncell, 26, 60.

71. Sextett für 2 Klarinetten, 2 Hörner und 2 Fagotte, 182.

72a. Leonore, Oper, 34, 68, 121, 126, 135, 140, 164, 165, 166, 169, 175, 180.

73. Konzert für Pianoforte mit Begleitung des Orchesters, 126, 137, 179.

74. Quartett für 2 Violinen, Bratsche und Violoncell, 26, 51, 55, 68, 109, 132.

75. II. 'Neue Liebe, neues Leben', für 1 Singstimme mit Begleitung, 172.

76. Variationen *D* dur für Pianoforte, 142.

79. Sonatine für Pianoforte, 89, 175.

80. Phantasie für Pianoforte, Chor und Orchester, 166, 180.

82. III, IV. 'L'amante impaziente', Ariette mit Begleitung des Pianoforte, 179.

83. I. 'Wonne der Wehmut', für 1 Singstimme mit Begleitung des Pianoforte, 168.

83. III. 'Mit einem gemalten Band', für 1 Singstimme mit Begleitung des Pianoforte, 105.

84. I. 'Die Trommel gerührt', Lied aus Egmont, 184.

89. Polonaise für Pianoforte, 180.

90. Sonate für Pianoforte, 5, 38, 104.

91. Wellingtons Sieg oder die Schlacht bei Vittoria, für Orchester, 180.

92. VII. Symphonie, 55, 81, 88, 120.

93. VIII. Symphonie, 6, 16, 18, 21, 64, 66, 70, 87.

95. Quartett für 2 Violinen, Bratsche und Violoncell, 55, 182.

96. Sonate für Pianoforte und Violine, 25, 33, 76, 171.

97. Trio für Pianoforte, Violine und Violoncell, 54, 77, 86, 87, 148.

98. 'An die ferne Geliebte', für 1 Singstimme mit Begleitung des Pianoforte, 6, 38, 158.

101. Sonate für Pianoforte, 64, 83, 112, 138, 180.

102. I. Sonate für Pianoforte und Violoncell, 7.

Op.

102. II. Sonate für Pianoforte und Violoncell, 128.

103. Oktett für 2 Oboen, 2 Klarinetten, 2 Hörner und 2 Fagotte, 55, 186.

106. Sonate für Pianoforte, 8, 11, 17, 20, 28, 40, 50, 66, 102, 138, 144.

108. XI. Schottisches Lied, 178.

109. Sonate für Pianoforte, 21, 30, 50, 104.

110. Sonate für Pianoforte, 112, 114.

111. Sonate für Pianoforte, 142, 149.

113. Die Ruinen von Athen, 135, 137, 165, 178, 180.

115. Ouvertüre C dur, 99, 149, 163, 180, 182.

121b. 'Opferlied', für 1 Sopranstimme mit Chor und Orchesterbegleitung, 149, 163, 175.
'Opferlied', für 1 Singstimme mit Begleitung des Pianoforte, 149, 163, 175.

122. 'Bundeslied', für Solo, Chor und Blasinstrumente, 165.

123. Missa solemnis, 112, 136, 145, 149, 151, 153, 165, 169, 184.

124. Ouvertüre 'Die Weihe des Hauses', 128.

125. IX. Symphonie, 7, 15, 55, 58, 74, 77, 102, 112, 145, 149, 153, 167, 175, 184.

126. 6 Bagatellen für Pianoforte, 60, 94, 103, 133, 176.

127. Quartett für 2 Violinen, Bratsche und Violoncell, 7, 51, 106, 152, 158, 181.

130. Quartett für 2 Violinen, Bratsche und Violoncell, 25, 33, 41, 51, 109, 129, 130, 171, 173, 176.

131. Quartett für 2 Violinen, Bratsche und Violoncell, 10, 17, 25, 55, 96, 111, 158.

132. Quartett für 2 Violinen, Bratsche und Violoncell, 8, 15, 42, 58, 61, 89, 103, 129, 155, 178.

133. Fuge für 2 Violinen, Bratsche und Violoncell, 112, 129.

135. Quartett für 2 Violinen, Bratsche und Violoncell, 33, 110.

138. Ouvertüre C dur zur Leonore, 92.

Variationen G dur für Pianoforte, 124, 142.

Variationen über 'Une fièvre brûlante' für Pianoforte, 142.

Andante F dur für Pianoforte, 128, 138, 183.

'Lustig-Traurig', 2 Stücke für Pianoforte, 181.

Marsch F dur für Orchester, 129, 180.

Militärmarsch D dur für Orchester, 180.

Triumphmarsch *C* dur für Orchester, 180.

'Der freie Mann', für 1 Singstimme, Chor und Begleitung des Pianoforte, 136, 137.

'Ich war bei Chloe', für 1 Singstimme mit Begleitung des Pianoforte, 149.

'Sehnsucht' (Die stille Nacht), für 1 Singstimme mit Begleitung des Pianoforte, 175.

'Sehnsucht' (Nur wer die Sehnsucht kennt), für 1 Singstimme mit Begleitung des Pianoforte, 179.

'Seufzer eines Ungeliebten und Gegenliebe', für 1 Singstimme mit Begleitung des Pianoforte, 166, 180.

Schottische, irische ... Lieder, 178.

Trauerkantate, 178.

INDEX OF NAMES

Altmann, W., 55.
Amenda, K., 157, 169.
Anschütz, H., 147.

Bach, J. S., 44, 102, 114.
Bach, K. Ph. E., 53.
Becking, G., 2, 26, 54, 67.
Beethoven, L. van.
Beethovenhaus, Bonn, 36, 94, 124, 159.
Beyschlag, A., 173.
Brahms, J., 29, 30, 116, 162, 170.
Braun von Braunthal, 131.
Brentano, Bettina, 131.
Breuning, G. von, 147, 157.
Bridgetower, G. A. P., 130.
Bursy, K. von, 117, 130.
Busoni, F., 156.

Czerny, K., 84, 160.

Deutsch, O. E., 156.
Duncker, J. F. L., 181.

Essner, W., 6, 113.

Fischer, W., 4, 44, 45, 46, 51, 61, 76, 92, 124.
Friedländer, M., 2, 162.

Gal, H., 2, 4, 29, 31, 35, 38, 39, 40, 50, 69, 100, 178, 182.
Goethe, Wolfg. von, 24, 162, 179.
Graf, M., 158, 187.

Händel, G. F., 156.
Haydn, J., 35, 53, 113, 188.
Helm, Th., 103.
Hennig, R., 181.
Heuss, A., 147, 149.
Hoffmann, E. T. A., 156.

Jahn, O., 1.
Jalowetz, H., 4, 28, 53.
Joachim, J., 32.

Kerst, F., 160.
Kinsky, G., 179.
Klopstock, F. G., 174.
Knab, A., 114.
Kotzebue, A. von, 179.
Kurth, E., 102.

Leitzmann, A., 8, 128, 129, 147, 162.
Lorenz, A., 66.

Meumann, E., 150, 155.
Mies, P., 3, 16, 24, 30, 65, 68, 114, 116, 162, 170.
Molnar, A., 167.
Moser, A., 32.
Mozart, W. A., 29, 31, 36, 52, 188.
Müller-Reuter, Th., 7, 84.

Naumann, E., 16, 27.
Nottebohm, G.

Oppel, R., 53.
Orel, A., 55.

Pergolesi, G. B., 46.
Prieger, E., 34, 35, 68, 164, 169.

Riemann, H., 7, 51, 61, 63, 92, 124, 147, 171.
Ries, F., 8, 128, 157.
Rochlitz, F., 162, 174.

Schenker, H., 1, 3, 112, 142.
Schindler, A., 148, 163, 170, 174.
Schlösser, L., 129, 131, 158, 159.

197

Schmitz, A., 34, 57, 91, 94, 100,
159, 187.
Schubart, C. F. D., 174.
Schubert, F., 24, 131, 156, 188.
Schumann, R., 1, 24, 55, 160,
188.
Seyfried, J. von, 157, 162.
Sondheimer, R., 52.
Spitta, Ph., 147, 162, 188.
Stephani, H., 174.
Stumpff, J. A., 160.

Thayer-Deiters-Riemann, 3, 103,
124, 128, 129, 130, 158, 159,
160, 163, 177, 178.
Thomson, G., 178.

Utitz, E., 69.

Wagner, R., 66.
Wetzel, H., 102, 103.
Wetzler, H. H., 148.
Wolf, H., 24.

A CATALOGUE OF SELECTED DOVER BOOKS
IN ALL FIELDS OF INTEREST

A CATALOGUE OF SELECTED DOVER BOOKS
IN ALL FIELDS OF INTEREST

AMERICA'S OLD MASTERS, James T. Flexner. Four men emerged unexpectedly from provincial 18th century America to leadership in European art: Benjamin West, J. S. Copley, C. R. Peale, Gilbert Stuart. Brilliant coverage of lives and contributions. Revised, 1967 edition. 69 plates. 365pp. of text.

21806-6 Paperbound $3.00

FIRST FLOWERS OF OUR WILDERNESS: AMERICAN PAINTING, THE COLONIAL PERIOD, James T. Flexner. Painters, and regional painting traditions from earliest Colonial times up to the emergence of Copley, West and Peale Sr., Foster, Gustavus Hesselius, Feke, John Smibert and many anonymous painters in the primitive manner. Engaging presentation, with 162 illustrations. xxii + 368pp.

22180-6 Paperbound $3.50

THE LIGHT OF DISTANT SKIES: AMERICAN PAINTING, 1760-1835, James T. Flexner. The great generation of early American painters goes to Europe to learn and to teach: West, Copley, Gilbert Stuart and others. Allston, Trumbull, Morse; also contemporary American painters—primitives, derivatives, academics—who remained in America. 102 illustrations. xiii + 306pp. 22179-2 Paperbound $3.00

A HISTORY OF THE RISE AND PROGRESS OF THE ARTS OF DESIGN IN THE UNITED STATES, William Dunlap. Much the richest mine of information on early American painters, sculptors, architects, engravers, miniaturists, etc. The only source of information for scores of artists, the major primary source for many others. Unabridged reprint of rare original 1834 edition, with new introduction by James T. Flexner, and 394 new illustrations. Edited by Rita Weiss. 6⅝ x 9⅝.

21695-0, 21696-9, 21697-7 Three volumes, Paperbound $13.50

EPOCHS OF CHINESE AND JAPANESE ART, Ernest F. Fenollosa. From primitive Chinese art to the 20th century, thorough history, explanation of every important art period and form, including Japanese woodcuts; main stress on China and Japan, but Tibet, Korea also included. Still unexcelled for its detailed, rich coverage of cultural background, aesthetic elements, diffusion studies, particularly of the historical period. 2nd, 1913 edition. 242 illustrations. lii + 439pp. of text.

20364-6, 20365-4 Two volumes, Paperbound $6.00

THE GENTLE ART OF MAKING ENEMIES, James A. M. Whistler. Greatest wit of his day deflates Oscar Wilde, Ruskin, Swinburne; strikes back at inane critics, exhibitions, art journalism; aesthetics of impressionist revolution in most striking form. Highly readable classic by great painter. Reproduction of edition designed by Whistler. Introduction by Alfred Werner. xxxvi + 334pp.

21875-9 Paperbound $2.50

JOHANN SEBASTIAN BACH, Philipp Spitta. One of the great classics of musicology, this definitive analysis of Bach's music (and life) has never been surpassed. Lucid, nontechnical analyses of hundreds of pieces (30 pages devoted to St. Matthew Passion, 26 to B Minor Mass). Also includes major analysis of 18th-century music. 450 musical examples. 40-page musical supplement. Total of xx + 1799pp.
(EUK) 22278-0, 22279-9 Two volumes, Clothbound $15.00

MOZART AND HIS PIANO CONCERTOS, Cuthbert Girdlestone. The only full-length study of an important area of Mozart's creativity. Provides detailed analyses of all 23 concertos, traces inspirational sources. 417 musical examples. Second edition. 509pp.
(USO) 21271-8 Paperbound $3.50

THE PERFECT WAGNERITE: A COMMENTARY ON THE NIBLUNG'S RING, George Bernard Shaw. Brilliant and still relevant criticism in remarkable essays on Wagner's Ring cycle, Shaw's ideas on political and social ideology behind the plots, role of Leitmotifs, vocal requisites, etc. Prefaces. xxi + 136pp.
21707-8 Paperbound $1.50

DON GIOVANNI, W. A. Mozart. Complete libretto, modern English translation; biographies of composer and librettist; accounts of early performances and critical reaction. Lavishly illustrated. All the material you need to understand and appreciate this great work. Dover Opera Guide and Libretto Series; translated and introduced by Ellen Bleiler. 92 illustrations. 209pp.
21134-7 Paperbound $1.50

HIGH FIDELITY SYSTEMS: A LAYMAN'S GUIDE, Roy F. Allison. All the basic information you need for setting up your own audio system: high fidelity and stereo record players, tape records, F.M. Connections, adjusting tone arm, cartridge, checking needle alignment, positioning speakers, phasing speakers, adjusting hums, trouble-shooting, maintenance, and similar topics. Enlarged 1965 edition. More than 50 charts, diagrams, photos. iv + 91pp.
21514-8 Paperbound $1.25

REPRODUCTION OF SOUND, Edgar Villchur. Thorough coverage for laymen of high fidelity systems, reproducing systems in general, needles, amplifiers, preamps, loudspeakers, feedback, explaining physical background. "A rare talent for making technicalities vividly comprehensible," R. Darrell, *High Fidelity*. 69 figures. iv + 92pp.
21515-6 Paperbound $1.00

HEAR ME TALKIN' TO YA: THE STORY OF JAZZ AS TOLD BY THE MEN WHO MADE IT, Nat Shapiro and Nat Hentoff. Louis Armstrong, Fats Waller, Jo Jones, Clarence Williams, Billy Holiday, Duke Ellington, Jelly Roll Morton and dozens of other jazz greats tell how it was in Chicago's South Side, New Orleans, depression Harlem and the modern West Coast as jazz was born and grew. xvi + 429pp.
21726-4 Paperbound $2.50

FABLES OF AESOP, translated by Sir Roger L'Estrange. A reproduction of the very rare 1931 Paris edition; a selection of the most interesting fables, together with 50 imaginative drawings by Alexander Calder. v + 128pp. 6½x9¼.
21780-9 Paperbound $1.25

POEMS OF ANNE BRADSTREET, edited with an introduction by Robert Hutchinson. A new selection of poems by America's first poet and perhaps the first significant woman poet in the English language. 48 poems display her development in works of considerable variety—love poems, domestic poems, religious meditations, formal elegies, "quaternions," etc. Notes, bibliography. viii + 222pp.

22160-1 Paperbound $2.00

THREE GOTHIC NOVELS: THE CASTLE OF OTRANTO BY HORACE WALPOLE; VATHEK BY WILLIAM BECKFORD; THE VAMPYRE BY JOHN POLIDORI, WITH FRAGMENT OF A NOVEL BY LORD BYRON, edited by E. F. Bleiler. The first Gothic novel, by Walpole; the finest Oriental tale in English, by Beckford; powerful Romantic supernatural story in versions by Polidori and Byron. All extremely important in history of literature; all still exciting, packed with supernatural thrills, ghosts, haunted castles, magic, etc. xl + 291pp.

21232-7 Paperbound $2.50

THE BEST TALES OF HOFFMANN, E. T. A. Hoffmann. 10 of Hoffmann's most important stories, in modern re-editings of standard translations: Nutcracker and the King of Mice, Signor Formica, Automata, The Sandman, Rath Krespel, The Golden Flowerpot, Master Martin the Cooper, The Mines of Falun, The King's Betrothed, A New Year's Eve Adventure. 7 illustrations by Hoffmann. Edited by E. F. Bleiler. xxxix + 419pp. 21793-0 Paperbound $3.00

GHOST AND HORROR STORIES OF AMBROSE BIERCE, Ambrose Bierce. 23 strikingly modern stories of the horrors latent in the human mind: The Eyes of the Panther, The Damned Thing, An Occurrence at Owl Creek Bridge, An Inhabitant of Carcosa, etc., plus the dream-essay, Visions of the Night. Edited by E. F. Bleiler. xxii + 199pp. 20767-6 Paperbound $1.50

BEST GHOST STORIES OF J. S. LEFANU, J. Sheridan LeFanu. Finest stories by Victorian master often considered greatest supernatural writer of all. Carmilla, Green Tea, The Haunted Baronet, The Familiar, and 12 others. Most never before available in the U. S. A. Edited by E. F. Bleiler. 8 illustrations from Victorian publications. xvii + 467pp. 20415-4 Paperbound $3.00

MATHEMATICAL FOUNDATIONS OF INFORMATION THEORY, A. I. Khinchin. Comprehensive introduction to work of Shannon, McMillan, Feinstein and Khinchin, placing these investigations on a rigorous mathematical basis. Covers entropy concept in probability theory, uniqueness theorem, Shannon's inequality, ergodic sources, the E property, martingale concept, noise, Feinstein's fundamental lemma, Shanon's first and second theorems. Translated by R. A. Silverman and M. D. Friedman. iii + 120pp. 60434-9 Paperbound $1.75

SEVEN SCIENCE FICTION NOVELS, H. G. Wells. The standard collection of the great novels. Complete, unabridged. *First Men in the Moon, Island of Dr. Moreau, War of the Worlds, Food of the Gods, Invisible Man, Time Machine, In the Days of the Comet.* Not only science fiction fans, but every educated person owes it to himself to read these novels. 1015pp 20264-X Clothbound $5.00

EAST O' THE SUN AND WEST O' THE MOON, George W. Dasent. Considered the best of all translations of these Norwegian folk tales, this collection has been enjoyed by generations of children (and folklorists too). Includes True and Untrue, Why the Sea is Salt, East O' the Sun and West O' the Moon, Why the Bear is Stumpy-Tailed, Boots and the Troll, The Cock and the Hen, Rich Peter the Pedlar, and 52 more. The only edition with all 59 tales. 77 illustrations by Erik Werenskiold and Theodor Kittelsen. xv + 418pp. 22521-6 Paperbound $3.50

GOOPS AND HOW TO BE THEM, Gelett Burgess. Classic of tongue-in-cheek humor, masquerading as etiquette book. 87 verses, twice as many cartoons, show mischievous Goops as they demonstrate to children virtues of table manners, neatness, courtesy, etc. Favorite for generations. viii + 88pp. 6½ x 9¼. 22233-0 Paperbound $1.25

ALICE'S ADVENTURES UNDER GROUND, Lewis Carroll. The first version, quite different from the final *Alice in Wonderland,* printed out by Carroll himself with his own illustrations. Complete facsimile of the "million dollar" manuscript Carroll gave to Alice Liddell in 1864. Introduction by Martin Gardner. viii + 96pp. Title and dedication pages in color. 21482-6 Paperbound $1.25

THE BROWNIES, THEIR BOOK, Palmer Cox. Small as mice, cunning as foxes, exuberant and full of mischief, the Brownies go to the zoo, toy shop, seashore, circus, etc., in 24 verse adventures and 266 illustrations. Long a favorite, since their first appearance in St. Nicholas Magazine. xi + 144pp. 6⅝ x 9¼. 21265-3 Paperbound $1.75

SONGS OF CHILDHOOD, Walter De La Mare. Published (under the pseudonym Walter Ramal) when De La Mare was only 29, this charming collection has long been a favorite children's book. A facsimile of the first edition in paper, the 47 poems capture the simplicity of the nursery rhyme and the ballad, including such lyrics as I Met Eve, Tartary, The Silver Penny. vii + 106pp. 21972-0 Paperbound $1.25

THE COMPLETE NONSENSE OF EDWARD LEAR, Edward Lear. The finest 19th-century humorist-cartoonist in full: all nonsense limericks, zany alphabets, Owl and Pussycat, songs, nonsense botany, and more than 500 illustrations by Lear himself. Edited by Holbrook Jackson. xxix + 287pp. (USO) 20167-8 Paperbound $2.00

BILLY WHISKERS: THE AUTOBIOGRAPHY OF A GOAT, Frances Trego Montgomery. A favorite of children since the early 20th century, here are the escapades of that rambunctious, irresistible and mischievous goat—Billy Whiskers. Much in the spirit of *Peck's Bad Boy,* this is a book that children never tire of reading or hearing. All the original familiar illustrations by W. H. Fry are included: 6 color plates, 18 black and white drawings. 159pp. 22345-0 Paperbound $2.00

MOTHER GOOSE MELODIES. Faithful republication of the fabulously rare Munroe and Francis "copyright 1833" Boston edition—the most important Mother Goose collection, usually referred to as the "original." Familiar rhymes plus many rare ones, with wonderful old woodcut illustrations. Edited by E. F. Bleiler. 128pp. 4½ x 6⅜. 22577-1 Paperbound $1.25

THE ARCHITECTURE OF COUNTRY HOUSES, Andrew J. Downing. Together with Vaux's *Villas and Cottages* this is the basic book for Hudson River Gothic architecture of the middle Victorian period. Full, sound discussions of general aspects of housing, architecture, style, decoration, furnishing, together with scores of detailed house plans, illustrations of specific buildings, accompanied by full text. Perhaps the most influential single American architectural book. 1850 edition. Introduction by J. Stewart Johnson. 321 figures, 34 architectural designs. xvi + 560pp.
22003-6 Paperbound $4.00

LOST EXAMPLES OF COLONIAL ARCHITECTURE, John Mead Howells. Full-page photographs of buildings that have disappeared or been so altered as to be denatured, including many designed by major early American architects. 245 plates. xvii + 248pp. 7⅞ x 10¾. 21143-6 Paperbound $3.50

DOMESTIC ARCHITECTURE OF THE AMERICAN COLONIES AND OF THE EARLY REPUBLIC, Fiske Kimball. Foremost architect and restorer of Williamsburg and Monticello covers nearly 200 homes between 1620-1825. Architectural details, construction, style features, special fixtures, floor plans, etc. Generally considered finest work in its area. 219 illustrations of houses, doorways, windows, capital mantels. xx + 314pp. 7⅞ x 10¾. 21743-4 Paperbound $4.00

EARLY AMERICAN ROOMS: 1650-1858, edited by Russell Hawes Kettell. Tour of 12 rooms, each representative of a different era in American history and each furnished, decorated, designed and occupied in the style of the era. 72 plans and elevations, 8-page color section, etc., show fabrics, wall papers, arrangements, etc. Full descriptive text. xvii + 200pp. of text. 8⅜ x 11¼.
21633-0 Paperbound $5.00

THE FITZWILLIAM VIRGINAL BOOK, edited by J. Fuller Maitland and W. B. Squire. Full modern printing of famous early 17th-century ms. volume of 300 works by Morley, Byrd, Bull, Gibbons, etc. For piano or other modern keyboard instrument; easy to read format. xxxvi + 938pp. 8⅜ x 11.
21068-5, 21069-3 Two volumes, Paperbound $10.00

KEYBOARD MUSIC, Johann Sebastian Bach. Bach Gesellschaft edition. A rich selection of Bach's masterpieces for the harpsichord: the six English Suites, six French Suites, the six Partitas (Clavierübung part I), the Goldberg Variations (Clavierübung part IV), the fifteen Two-Part Inventions and the fifteen Three-Part Sinfonias. Clearly reproduced on large sheets with ample margins; eminently playable. vi + 312pp. 8⅛ x 11. 22360-4 Paperbound $5.00

THE MUSIC OF BACH: AN INTRODUCTION, Charles Sanford Terry. A fine, nontechnical introduction to Bach's music, both instrumental and vocal. Covers organ music, chamber music, passion music, other types. Analyzes themes, developments, innovations. x + 114pp. 21075-8 Paperbound $1.25

BEETHOVEN AND HIS NINE SYMPHONIES, Sir George Grove. Noted British musicologist provides best history, analysis, commentary on symphonies. Very thorough, rigorously accurate; necessary to both advanced student and amateur music lover. 436 musical passages. vii + 407 pp. 20334-4 Paperbound $2.75

A HISTORY OF COSTUME, Carl Köhler. Definitive history, based on surviving pieces of clothing primarily, and paintings, statues, etc. secondarily. Highly readable text, supplemented by 594 illustrations of costumes of the ancient Mediterranean peoples, Greece and Rome, the Teutonic prehistoric period; costumes of the Middle Ages, Renaissance, Baroque, 18th and 19th centuries. Clear, measured patterns are provided for many clothing articles. Approach is practical throughout. Enlarged by Emma von Sichart. 464pp. 21030-8 Paperbound $3.50

ORIENTAL RUGS, ANTIQUE AND MODERN, Walter A. Hawley. A complete and authoritative treatise on the Oriental rug—where they are made, by whom and how, designs and symbols, characteristics in detail of the six major groups, how to distinguish them and how to buy them. Detailed technical data is provided on periods, weaves, warps, wefts, textures, sides, ends and knots, although no technical background is required for an understanding. 11 color plates, 80 halftones, 4 maps. vi + 320pp. 6⅛ x 9⅛. 22366-3 Paperbound $5.00

TEN BOOKS ON ARCHITECTURE, Vitruvius. By any standards the most important book on architecture ever written. Early Roman discussion of aesthetics of building, construction methods, orders, sites, and every other aspect of architecture has inspired, instructed architecture for about 2,000 years. Stands behind Palladio, Michelangelo, Bramante, Wren, countless others. Definitive Morris H. Morgan translation. 68 illustrations. xii + 331pp. 20645-9 Paperbound $3.50

THE FOUR BOOKS OF ARCHITECTURE, Andrea Palladio. Translated into every major Western European language in the two centuries following its publication in 1570, this has been one of the most influential books in the history of architecture. Complete reprint of the 1738 Isaac Ware edition. New introduction by Adolf Placzek, Columbia Univ. 216 plates. xxii + 110pp. of text. 9½ x 12¾. 21308-0 Clothbound $10.00

STICKS AND STONES: A STUDY OF AMERICAN ARCHITECTURE AND CIVILIZATION, Lewis Mumford.One of the great classics of American cultural history. American architecture from the medieval-inspired earliest forms to the early 20th century; evolution of structure and style, and reciprocal influences on environment. 21 photographic illustrations. 238pp. 20202-X Paperbound $2.00

THE AMERICAN BUILDER'S COMPANION, Asher Benjamin. The most widely used early 19th century architectural style and source book, for colonial up into Greek Revival periods. Extensive development of geometry of carpentering, construction of sashes, frames, doors, stairs; plans and elevations of domestic and other buildings. Hundreds of thousands of houses were built according to this book, now invaluable to historians, architects, restorers, etc. 1827 edition. 59 plates. 114pp. 7⅞ x 10¾. 22236-5 Paperbound $3.50

DUTCH HOUSES IN THE HUDSON VALLEY BEFORE 1776, Helen Wilkinson Reynolds. The standard survey of the Dutch colonial house and outbuildings, with constructional features, decoration, and local history associated with individual homesteads. Introduction by Franklin D. Roosevelt. Map. 150 illustrations. 469pp. 6⅝ x 9¼. 21469-9 Paperbound $4.00

PLANETS, STARS AND GALAXIES: DESCRIPTIVE ASTRONOMY FOR BEGINNERS, A. E. Fanning. Comprehensive introductory survey of astronomy: the sun, solar system, stars, galaxies, universe, cosmology; up-to-date, including quasars, radio stars, etc. Preface by Prof. Donald Menzel. 24pp. of photographs. 189pp. 5¼ x 8¼.

21680-2 Paperbound $1.50

TEACH YOURSELF CALCULUS, P. Abbott. With a good background in algebra and trig, you can teach yourself calculus with this book. Simple, straightforward introduction to functions of all kinds, integration, differentiation, series, etc. "Students who are beginning to study calculus method will derive great help from this book." Faraday House Journal. 308pp.   20683-1 Clothbound $2.00

TEACH YOURSELF TRIGONOMETRY, P. Abbott. Geometrical foundations, indices and logarithms, ratios, angles, circular measure, etc. are presented in this sound, easy-to-use text. Excellent for the beginner or as a brush up, this text carries the student through the solution of triangles. 204pp.   20682-3 Clothbound $2.00

TEACH YOURSELF ANATOMY, David LeVay. Accurate, inclusive, profusely illustrated account of structure, skeleton, abdomen, muscles, nervous system, glands, brain, reproductive organs, evolution. "Quite the best and most readable account,' Medical Officer. 12 color plates. 164 figures. 311pp. 4¾ x 7.

21651-9 Clothbound $2.50

TEACH YOURSELF PHYSIOLOGY, David LeVay. Anatomical, biochemical bases; digestive, nervous, endocrine systems; metabolism; respiration; muscle; excretion; temperature control; reproduction. "Good elementary exposition," The Lancet. 6 color plates. 44 illustrations. 208pp. 4¼ x 7.   21658-6 Clothbound $2.50

THE FRIENDLY STARS, Martha Evans Martin. Classic has taught naked-eye observation of stars, planets to hundreds of thousands, still not surpassed for charm, lucidity, adequacy. Completely updated by Professor Donald H. Menzel, Harvard Observatory. 25 illustrations. 16 x 30 chart. x + 147pp.   21099-5 Paperbound $1.25

MUSIC OF THE SPHERES: THE MATERIAL UNIVERSE FROM ATOM TO QUASAR, SIMPLY EXPLAINED, Guy Murchie. Extremely broad, brilliantly written popular account begins with the solar system and reaches to dividing line between matter and nonmatter; latest understandings presented with exceptional clarity. Volume One: Planets, stars, galaxies, cosmology, geology, celestial mechanics, latest astronomical discoveries; Volume Two: Matter, atoms, waves, radiation, relativity, chemical action, heat, nuclear energy, quantum theory, music, light, color, probability, antimatter, antigravity, and similar topics. 319 figures. 1967 (second) edition. Total of xx + 644pp.   21809-0, 21810-4 Two volumes, Paperbound $5.00

OLD-TIME SCHOOLS AND SCHOOL BOOKS, Clifton Johnson. Illustrations and rhymes from early primers, abundant quotations from early textbooks, many anecdotes of school life enliven this study of elementary schools from Puritans to middle 19th century. Introduction by Carl Withers. 234 illustrations. xxxiii + 381pp.

21031-6 Paperbound $2.50

Two Little Savages; Being the Adventures of Two Boys Who Lived as Indians and What They Learned, Ernest Thompson Seton. Great classic of nature and boyhood provides a vast range of woodlore in most palatable form, a genuinely entertaining story. Two farm boys build a teepee in woods and live in it for a month, working out Indian solutions to living problems, star lore, birds and animals, plants, etc. 293 illustrations. vii + 286pp.

20985-7 Paperbound $2.50

Peter Piper's Practical Principles of Plain & Perfect Pronunciation. Alliterative jingles and tongue-twisters of surprising charm, that made their first appearance in America about 1830. Republished in full with the spirited woodcut illustrations from this earliest American edition. 32pp. 4½ x 6⅜.

22560-7 Paperbound $1.00

Science Experiments and Amusements for Children, Charles Vivian. 73 easy experiments, requiring only materials found at home or easily available, such as candles, coins, steel wool, etc.; illustrate basic phenomena like vacuum, simple chemical reaction, etc. All safe. Modern, well-planned. Formerly *Science Games for Children*. 102 photos, numerous drawings. 96pp. 6⅛ x 9¼.

21856-2 Paperbound $1.25

An Introduction to Chess Moves and Tactics Simply Explained, Leonard Barden. Informal intermediate introduction, quite strong in explaining reasons for moves. Covers basic material, tactics, important openings, traps, positional play in middle game, end game. Attempts to isolate patterns and recurrent configurations. Formerly *Chess*. 58 figures. 102pp.   (USO) 21210-6 Paperbound $1.25

Lasker's Manual of Chess, Dr. Emanuel Lasker. Lasker was not only one of the five great World Champions, he was also one of the ablest expositors, theorists, and analysts. In many ways, his Manual, permeated with his philosophy of battle, filled with keen insights, is one of the greatest works ever written on chess. Filled with analyzed games by the great players. A single-volume library that will profit almost any chess player, beginner or master. 308 diagrams. xli x 349pp.

20640-8 Paperbound $2.75

The Master Book of Mathematical Recreations, Fred Schuh. In opinion of many the finest work ever prepared on mathematical puzzles, stunts, recreations; exhaustively thorough explanations of mathematics involved, analysis of effects, citation of puzzles and games. Mathematics involved is elementary. Translated by F. Göbel. 194 figures. xxiv + 430pp.   22134-2 Paperbound $3.00

Mathematics, Magic and Mystery, Martin Gardner. Puzzle editor for Scientific American explains mathematics behind various mystifying tricks: card tricks, stage "mind reading," coin and match tricks, counting out games, geometric dissections, etc. Probability sets, theory of numbers clearly explained. Also provides more than 400 tricks, guaranteed to work, that you can do. 135 illustrations. xii + 176pp.

20338-2 Paperbound $1.50

THE PRINCIPLES OF PSYCHOLOGY, William James. The famous long course, complete and unabridged. Stream of thought, time perception, memory, experimental methods—these are only some of the concerns of a work that was years ahead of its time and still valid, interesting, useful. 94 figures. Total of xviii + 1391pp.
20381-6, 20382-4 Two volumes, Paperbound $8.00

THE STRANGE STORY OF THE QUANTUM, Banesh Hoffmann. Non-mathematical but thorough explanation of work of Planck, Einstein, Bohr, Pauli, de Broglie, Schrödinger, Heisenberg, Dirac, Feynman, etc. No technical background needed. "Of books attempting such an account, this is the best," Henry Margenau, Yale. 40-page "Postscript 1959." xii + 285pp. 20518-5 Paperbound $2.00

THE RISE OF THE NEW PHYSICS, A. d'Abro. Most thorough explanation in print of central core of mathematical physics, both classical and modern; from Newton to Dirac and Heisenberg. Both history and exposition; philosophy of science, causality, explanations of higher mathematics, analytical mechanics, electromagnetism, thermodynamics, phase rule, special and general relativity, matrices. No higher mathematics needed to follow exposition, though treatment is elementary to intermediate in level. Recommended to serious student who wishes verbal understanding. 97 illustrations. xvii + 982pp. 20003-5, 20004-3 Two volumes, Paperbound $6.00

GREAT IDEAS OF OPERATIONS RESEARCH, Jagjit Singh. Easily followed non-technical explanation of mathematical tools, aims, results: statistics, linear programming, game theory, queueing theory, Monte Carlo simulation, etc. Uses only elementary mathematics. Many case studies, several analyzed in detail. Clarity, breadth make this excellent for specialist in another field who wishes background. 41 figures. x + 228pp. 21886-4 Paperbound $2.50

GREAT IDEAS OF MODERN MATHEMATICS: THEIR NATURE AND USE, Jagjit Singh. Internationally famous expositor, winner of Unesco's Kalinga Award for science popularization explains verbally such topics as differential equations, matrices, groups, sets, transformations, mathematical logic and other important modern mathematics, as well as use in physics, astrophysics, and similar fields. Superb exposition for layman, scientist in other areas. viii + 312pp.
20587-8 Paperbound $2.50

GREAT IDEAS IN INFORMATION THEORY, LANGUAGE AND CYBERNETICS, Jagjit Singh. The analog and digital computers, how they work, how they are like and unlike the human brain, the men who developed them, their future applications, computer terminology. An essential book for today, even for readers with little math. Some mathematical demonstrations included for more advanced readers. 118 figures. Tables. ix + 338pp. 21694-2 Paperbound $2.50

CHANCE, LUCK AND STATISTICS, Horace C. Levinson. Non-mathematical presentation of fundamentals of probability theory and science of statistics and their applications. Games of chance, betting odds, misuse of statistics, normal and skew distributions, birth rates, stock speculation, insurance. Enlarged edition. Formerly "The Science of Chance." xiii + 357pp. 21007-3 Paperbound $2.50

AMERICAN FOOD AND GAME FISHES, David S. Jordan and Barton W. Evermann. Definitive source of information, detailed and accurate enough to enable the sportsman and nature lover to identify conclusively some 1,000 species and sub-species of North American fish, sought for food or sport. Coverage of range, physiology, habits, life history, food value. Best methods of capture, interest to the angler, advice on bait, fly-fishing, etc. 338 drawings and photographs. 1 + 574pp. 6⅝ x 9⅜.

22383-1 Paperbound $4.50

THE FROG BOOK, Mary C. Dickerson. Complete with extensive finding keys, over 300 photographs, and an introduction to the general biology of frogs and toads, this is the classic non-technical study of Northeastern and Central species. 58 species; 290 photographs and 16 color plates. xvii + 253pp.

21973-9 Paperbound $4.00

THE MOTH BOOK: A GUIDE TO THE MOTHS OF NORTH AMERICA, William J. Holland. Classical study, eagerly sought after and used for the past 60 years. Clear identification manual to more than 2,000 different moths, largest manual in existence. General information about moths, capturing, mounting, classifying, etc., followed by species by species descriptions. 263 illustrations plus 48 color plates show almost every species, full size. 1968 edition, preface, nomenclature changes by A. E. Brower. xxiv + 479pp. of text. 6½ x 9¼.

21948-8 Paperbound $5.00

THE SEA-BEACH AT EBB-TIDE, Augusta Foote Arnold. Interested amateur can identify hundreds of marine plants and animals on coasts of North America; marine algae; seaweeds; squids; hermit crabs; horse shoe crabs; shrimps; corals; sea anemones; etc. Species descriptions cover: structure; food; reproductive cycle; size; shape; color; habitat; etc. Over 600 drawings. 85 plates. xii + 490pp.

21949-6 Paperbound $3.50

COMMON BIRD SONGS, Donald J. Borror. 33⅓ 12-inch record presents songs of 60 important birds of the eastern United States. A thorough, serious record which provides several examples for each bird, showing different types of song, individual variations, etc. Inestimable identification aid for birdwatcher. 32-page booklet gives text about birds and songs, with illustration for each bird.

21829-5 Record, book, album. Monaural. $2.75

FADS AND FALLACIES IN THE NAME OF SCIENCE, Martin Gardner. Fair, witty appraisal of cranks and quacks of science: Atlantis, Lemuria, hollow earth, flat earth, Velikovsky, orgone energy, Dianetics, flying saucers, Bridey Murphy, food fads, medical fads, perpetual motion, etc. Formerly "In the Name of Science." x + 363pp.

20394-8 Paperbound $2.00

HOAXES, Curtis D. MacDougall. Exhaustive, unbelievably rich account of great hoaxes: Locke's moon hoax, Shakespearean forgeries, sea serpents, Loch Ness monster, Cardiff giant, John Wilkes Booth's mummy, Disumbrationist school of art, dozens more; also journalism, psychology of hoaxing. 54 illustrations. xi + 338pp.

20465-0 Paperbound $2.75

How to Know the Wild Flowers, Mrs. William Starr Dana. This is the classical book of American wildflowers (of the Eastern and Central United States), used by hundreds of thousands. Covers over 500 species, arranged in extremely easy to use color and season groups. Full descriptions, much plant lore. This Dover edition is the fullest ever compiled, with tables of nomenclature changes. 174 full-page plates by M. Satterlee. xii + 418pp. 20332-8 Paperbound $2.75

Our Plant Friends and Foes, William Atherton DuPuy. History, economic importance, essential botanical information and peculiarities of 25 common forms of plant life are provided in this book in an entertaining and charming style. Covers food plants (potatoes, apples, beans, wheat, almonds, bananas, etc.), flowers (lily, tulip, etc.), trees (pine, oak, elm, etc.), weeds, poisonous mushrooms and vines, gourds, citrus fruits, cotton, the cactus family, and much more. 108 illustrations. xiv + 290pp. 22272-1 Paperbound $2.50

How to Know the Ferns, Frances T. Parsons. Classic survey of Eastern and Central ferns, arranged according to clear, simple identification key. Excellent introduction to greatly neglected nature area. 57 illustrations and 42 plates. xvi + 215pp. 20740-4 Paperbound $2.00

Manual of the Trees of North America, Charles S. Sargent. America's foremost dendrologist provides the definitive coverage of North American trees and tree-like shrubs. 717 species fully described and illustrated: exact distribution, down to township; full botanical description; economic importance; description of subspecies and races; habitat, growth data; similar material. Necessary to every serious student of tree-life. Nomenclature revised to present. Over 100 locating keys. 783 illustrations. lii + 934pp. 20277-1, 20278-X Two volumes, Paperbound $6.00

Our Northern Shrubs, Harriet L. Keeler. Fine non-technical reference work identifying more than 225 important shrubs of Eastern and Central United States and Canada. Full text covering botanical description, habitat, plant lore, is paralleled with 205 full-page photographs of flowering or fruiting plants. Nomenclature revised by Edward G. Voss. One of few works concerned with shrubs. 205 plates, 35 drawings. xxviii + 521pp. 21989-5 Paperbound $3.75

The Mushroom Handbook, Louis C. C. Krieger. Still the best popular handbook: full descriptions of 259 species, cross references to another 200. Extremely thorough text enables you to identify, know all about any mushroom you are likely to meet in eastern and central U. S. A.: habitat, luminescence, poisonous qualities, use, folklore, etc. 32 color plates show over 50 mushrooms, also 126 other illustrations. Finding keys. vii + 560pp. 21861-9 Paperbound $3.95

Handbook of Birds of Eastern North America, Frank M. Chapman. Still much the best single-volume guide to the birds of Eastern and Central United States. Very full coverage of 675 species, with descriptions, life habits, distribution, similar data. All descriptions keyed to two-page color chart. With this single volume the average birdwatcher needs no other books. 1931 revised edition. 195 illustrations. xxxvi + 581pp. 21489-3 Paperbound $4.50

MATHEMATICAL PUZZLES FOR BEGINNERS AND ENTHUSIASTS, Geoffrey Mott-Smith. 189 puzzles from easy to difficult—involving arithmetic, logic, algebra, properties of digits, probability, etc.—for enjoyment and mental stimulus. Explanation of mathematical principles behind the puzzles. 135 illustrations. viii + 248pp.

20198-8 Paperbound $1.75

PAPER FOLDING FOR BEGINNERS, William D. Murray and Francis J. Rigney. Easiest book on the market, clearest instructions on making interesting, beautiful origami. Sail boats, cups, roosters, frogs that move legs, bonbon boxes, standing birds, etc. 40 projects; more than 275 diagrams and photographs. 94pp.

20713-7 Paperbound $1.00

TRICKS AND GAMES ON THE POOL TABLE, Fred Herrmann. 79 tricks and games—some solitaires, some for two or more players, some competitive games—to entertain you between formal games. Mystifying shots and throws, unusual caroms, tricks involving such props as cork, coins, a hat, etc. Formerly *Fun on the Pool Table.* 77 figures. 95pp.

21814-7 Paperbound $1.00

HAND SHADOWS TO BE THROWN UPON THE WALL: A SERIES OF NOVEL AND AMUSING FIGURES FORMED BY THE HAND, Henry Bursill. Delightful picturebook from great-grandfather's day shows how to make 18 different hand shadows: a bird that flies, duck that quacks, dog that wags his tail, camel, goose, deer, boy, turtle, etc. Only book of its sort. vi + 33pp. 6½ x 9¼. 21779-5 Paperbound $1.00

WHITTLING AND WOODCARVING, E. J. Tangerman. 18th printing of best book on market. "If you can cut a potato you can carve" toys and puzzles, chains, chessmen, caricatures, masks, frames, woodcut blocks, surface patterns, much more. Information on tools, woods, techniques. Also goes into serious wood sculpture from Middle Ages to present, East and West. 464 photos, figures. x + 293pp.

20965-2 Paperbound $2.00

HISTORY OF PHILOSOPHY, Julián Marias. Possibly the clearest, most easily followed, best planned, most useful one-volume history of philosophy on the market; neither skimpy nor overfull. Full details on system of every major philosopher and dozens of less important thinkers from pre-Socratics up to Existentialism and later. Strong on many European figures usually omitted. Has gone through dozens of editions in Europe. 1966 edition, translated by Stanley Appelbaum and Clarence Strowbridge. xviii + 505pp. 21739-6 Paperbound $3.00

YOGA: A SCIENTIFIC EVALUATION, Kovoor T. Behanan. Scientific but non-technical study of physiological results of yoga exercises; done under auspices of Yale U. Relations to Indian thought, to psychoanalysis, etc. 16 photos. xxiii + 270pp.

20505-3 Paperbound $2.50

Prices subject to change without notice.
Available at your book dealer or write for free catalogue to Dept. GI, Dover Publications, Inc., 180 Varick St., N. Y., N. Y. 10014. Dover publishes more than 150 books each year on science, elementary and advanced mathematics, biology, music, art, literary history, social sciences and other areas.